LESSONS FROM THE NONPROFIT
BOARDROOM

DAN BUSBY AND JOHN PEARSON

ISBN: 978-1-936233-77-9

CONTENTS

Contents

APPRECIATION

Dan thanks and dedicates this book to the leaders, board chairs, and board members of nearly 2,200 ECFA members.

John thanks and dedicates this book to the long-suffering board chairs he served with over his 30 years as a ministry CEO. With grateful appreciation to: Wally Wilson, Bill Pearson, Larry Haslam, Phil Hook, Bob McDowell, Bob Kraning, Keith Hunt, Gary Fawver, Max Rice, Bill Hybels, Pat Clements, Mark Holbrook, Jim Gwinn, and Jerry White. (For the record, John is not related to his former board chair, Bill Pearson!)

INTRODUCTION

Raise your hand if you're actually reading this introduction and you're not related to Dan or John. We thought so. So for the three readers who dutifully started at the beginning of this book—thank you! We'll try to make this introduction short, informative, and perhaps inspirational.

When the two of us read books, we reinforce learning with pens and highlighters. John skims the chapter titles first and notes two or three interesting chapters for immediate reading. If those chapters are worth the time, he then reads the introduction. He also reinforces his learning style by making notes on the blank pages in the front of the book.

Dan, the author or co-author of more than 60 book editions, brings a CPA's analytical skills to his first look at a new book. He looks at the meat and potatoes content, yes, but he also scans the endnotes, index, layout, binding, cover art, and pithy quotations. Both of us love to read and learn and we have high expectations of the books we read—like you do.

We bring all that to this book, *Lessons From the Nonprofit Boardroom*. And frankly, we had so much fun writing it, we're a bit sad this publishing journey is completed. But before you jump in, here are several notes for your reading edification.

Dan and John wrote an equal number of chapters—but we're not telling which ones. (Guess!) Actually, the content of several lessons delivers major hints about the author.

Dan and his wife would like readers to know he did not write Lesson 12. We've changed most of the board member names and places to protect the innocent (and the guilty). However, individuals named to the Board Member Hall of Fame are real board members—and we salute them!

Dan estimates he's participated in more than 300 board meetings over the years as a board member, board chair, ministry leader, or CEO. John has endured almost 500 board meetings, including observing many meetings during the last 12 years as a board governance consultant. We both have many stories—more lessons from the boardroom—that we *cannot* share in this book!

Both of us are passionate—very passionate—about the need for greater effectiveness in boardrooms where God's work is being conducted. We're blessed by the hundreds of boards we've observed that do practice true Christ-centered governance. Yet we're grieved when ego, incompetence, and sometimes just laziness become the obstacles to effectiveness and extraordinary Kingdom outcomes.

We are grateful for the growing volume of boardroom resources (many highlighted in this book) that help boards focus on their "customer," mission and vision, policy issues, spiritual discernment, Kingdom outcomes, sustainability, and so much more. Today, every board member must be a lifelong learner.

We are prayerful that this book will be one of several catalysts your board will use to catch the vision for good governance. We are hopeful that you'll help foster a ripple effect of enriching boardroom experiences that honor God. Like many, we believe that "as the board goes, so goes the organization."

Okay. Raise your hand if you read this entire introduction. (Thank you!)

Dan Busby
Winchester, VA

John Pearson
San Clemente, CA

P.S. News Flash! At press time, we admitted this was so much fun, we're now writing *More Lessons From the Nonprofit Boardroom*. Watch for it next year!

PART 1:
THE POWERFUL IMPACT OF HIGHLY ENGAGED BOARDS

Leadership is a complex field and no one resource
can meet all the needs of every leader in every situation.[1]

Richard Kriegbaum

1 | WANTED: LIFELONG LEARNERS

Would you trust a surgeon who stopped learning?

My best friend is a person
who will give me a book I have not read.

Abraham Lincoln

Do we really need another book on board governance? Short answer: yes. And here's why.

Board members in Christ-centered organizations across the nation—and around the world—are increasingly taking their board roles seriously. Highly engaged board chairs and board members know that when they say yes to board service, they must continually increase their knowledge and competencies to fulfill this sacred calling.

The challenges of stewarding a ministry are complex. Prospective board members are asking probing questions before saying yes to board service. (And many are saying no.) Many current board members are realizing that *they don't know what they don't know.* Lifelong learning, coupled with more prayer and more discernment, is on the front burner.

Would you trust a surgeon who was not a lifelong learner?

Would you trust an airline pilot who relied on outdated training?

Do your organization's donors and volunteers feel safe in your hands? Why should they trust your ministry's board of directors? Is your board on top of the rapid changes that are affecting all ministries as well as the changing role of the board?

There's still much to learn, and our prayer is that this book will be a catalyst for a wider understanding of Christ-centered governance, and a deeper dependence on God.

Business adviser and author Ram Charan reminds board members, "The role of the board has unmistakably transitioned from passive governance to active leadership with a delicate balance of avoiding micromanaging. It's leadership as a group, not leadership by an appointed person." [1]

He adds, "With the right composition, a board can create value; with the wrong or inappropriate composition, it can easily destroy value."[2]

Is your board adding value or subtracting value? How do you know?

BoardSource, which seeks to inspire and support excellence in nonprofit governance, publishes a book with 85 questions for board members.[3] (Do you know the 85 answers?) Charan says there are 14 questions every board member needs to ask.[4] Management consultant Peter Drucker wrote that there are just five "most important questions" for nonprofits (but who's counting?).[5]

ECFA enhances trust in Christ-centered churches and ministries by establishing and applying *Seven Standards of Responsible Stewardship*™ to accredited organizations. (Does your board review those seven standards at least annually? Can you name three of them?)

So you see, yes, we need another book on board leadership. There is so much to learn, and *Lessons From the Nonprofit Boardroom* will help and encourage you. We'll also help you sort out the truly core issues in governance from the rest of the noise and clutter.

> *"Leaders have a responsibility before God to constantly get better, and one of the most reliable ways to do so is to read. Great leaders read frequently. They read voraciously."*

Lifelong learning is critical—especially for leaders and board members who steward God's work. So read what Bill Hybels, founder of Willow Creek Community Church, says about the knowledge gap:

> The older I get and the longer I lead, the wider my knowledge gap becomes and the more aware I am of all that I don't know about leadership. But then there's Romans 12:8, which says that I am to "lead diligently." How am I supposed to lead diligently when there is so much left to learn?

> Leaders have a responsibility before God to *constantly* get better, and one of the most reliable ways to do so is to read. Great leaders read frequently. They read voraciously. They read classics and new releases. They soak up lessons from the military, from academia, from politics, from nongovernmental organizations,

and from church leaders who are leading well. They refuse to let themselves off the hook in this regard, because they know that all great leaders read.[6]

Our prayer is that you will leverage the insights in *Lessons From the Nonprofit Boardroom* so that your board will lead with eternity in view.

BOARDROOM LESSON

Board service is not for the weak of heart.
In Christ-centered organizations, it is a sacred calling that requires prayer and discernment, deep engagement, and a heart to be a lifelong learner. This book will help you on this sacred journey to be a competent, committed, and God-honoring board member.

Board Action Steps:

○ **1. Review:** Check out the Study Guide on pages 207–208 and select one or two next steps for your board.

○ **2. Read:** *Owning Up: The 14 Questions Every Board Member Needs to Ask* by Ram Charan.

○ **3. Share:** Give a copy of *Lessons From the Nonprofit Boardroom* to every board member and senior team member. Invite at least one board member per board meeting to share an insight gleaned from the book.

Prayer: "Lord, Romans 12:8 says that I am to lead diligently. Give me a heart to be a lifelong learner in my leadership journey. Amen."

2 | ASK THE GOLD STANDARD QUESTION

A "pruning moment" can improve your board meetings.

Questions to Ask about Your Meetings

What ways are we spending time in these meetings that are good and helpful but not the best use of our time together? What do we do here that is sick and not getting well?[1]

Henry Cloud

Several years ago, I conducted one-on-one phone interviews with nine board members who served together on a ministry board. I asked each of them my favorite engagement question:

> You're driving away from a typical board meeting, and you say, "That was a great board meeting today!" Tell me, what happened at the board meeting to provoke that positive response?

I call this my gold standard question because the responses are always indicative of a board member's satisfaction level with his or her board experience.

Over the years, when I ask this question, board members with unsatisfactory experiences often respond:

- "No one asked me for advice, wisdom, counsel, or ideas."

- "The staff read aloud the reports that we already had read in advance."

- "Boring. Routine. Pure agony."

- "Clearly, I'm not needed at the board table. The CEO did all the talking."

- "There was no sense of the holy except the perfunctory bookend prayers."

Conversely, here's what highly committed, deeply engaged, thrilled-to-be-serving board members tell me:

- "Everyone's prepared. Everyone participates. Everyone prays. It's the best board I have ever served on."

- "It happens all the time! We've deleted the petty stuff and focus on the important agenda items only. And we're on target financially."

During one phone call, a board member outlined four primary ingredients of memorable board meetings. (I was the consultant, yet he was teaching the course!)

☑ 1. There is deep joy consistently in every meeting.

☑ 2. The board is focused on strategic issues.

☑ 3. Energetic discussions abound. "We're not looking for agreement; we're looking for insight. Spiritual insight."

☑ 4. There is solidarity. "We foster a board culture that eliminates the unhealthy giving up of personal beliefs for the sake of unity. Instead, we wait for the Spirit of God to speak."

Imagine! What if your board had frequent moments characterized by deep joy, strategic issues, spiritual insight, and waiting for God to speak?

> *"If we own it, we have to prune. If we don't, we have decided to own the other vision, the one we called average."*

Imagine! What if when your board members are driving or flying home, their post-meeting reflections were deeply satisfying?

How do you move from your same-old-same-old board meeting routine to a new level of board excellence? Perhaps it's time for your board to announce what Dr. Henry Cloud calls a "necessary ending."

Cloud, a leadership coach to CEOs and business executives as well as being a clinical psychologist, introduced a new term into the leadership lexicon: "the pruning moment."[2]

He defined the pruning moment as "that clarity of enlightenment when we become responsible for making the decision to own the vision or not. If we own it, we have to prune. If we don't, we have decided to own the other vision, the one we called average. It is a moment of truth that we encounter almost every day in many, many decisions."[3]

Has your board sunk into an average vision with mediocre meetings? Is it time for a pruning moment?

BOARDROOM LESSON

Some boards slowly, almost imperceptibly, descend into the same-old-same-old board meeting routine and settle for average. Others focus on intentional improvement and reach a new level of board excellence— and they ooze God-honoring joy to others!

Board Action Steps:

○ **1. Ask:** "Before we start this meeting, we'd like every board member to think back and tell us about a great board meeting you attended and why it was so memorable."[4]

○ **2. Evaluate:** Distribute a short evaluation survey at the end of each meeting that is reviewed by the executive committee or the governance committee.

○ **3. Read:** Ask your "Leaders Are Readers Champion" (see Lesson 38) to review the ten short chapters in the "Board and Committee Meetings" section of *The Nonprofit Board Answer Book.*[5]

Prayer: "Lord, we don't want better board meetings just to satisfy our personal needs or to meet some arbitrary human standard. We desire highly effective board meetings to impact eternity. Amen."

3 ASSESS YOUR BOARDROOM DEMEANOR AND ENGAGEMENT

Does anybody need to make amends?

Dear God, help me to speak cautiously.
Let me use the least words, the least intensity,
the least volume to be understood.
Help me voice my opinions with care, strength, and meekness.
Help me to say nothing degrading
and nothing that would draw lines of conflict unnecessarily.[1]

Dan Bolin

At an elders' meeting at Willow Creek Community Church, a powerful question from the board chair cut to the heart of what Christ-centered governance looks like.

In his book *The Power of a Whisper: Hearing God. Having the Guts to Respond.,*[2] Bill Hybels, senior pastor of Willow Creek, shares a transparent story about the closing moments of one elders' meeting.

"In typical fashion the chairman of our board led us in a quick assessment of our demeanor and participation that evening. He asked, 'Does anybody need to make amends for anything, clarify a point, or apologize for a wrongdoing of any kind?'"

Hybels raised his hand—and his credibility—by confessing to a playful but inappropriate comment made earlier to a new elder. The elder was not offended and knew Bill was joking.

Yet this from Hybels: "I got a subtle flag in my spirit after I made that wisecrack," he admitted, "so I want to stick with the apology and ask your forgiveness here tonight."

That's just one of dozens of gems that eloquently illustrate the book's title. For me, this ranks on my top-five list of what distinguishes Christ-centered governance from the garden-variety type of boards that are content with "Let's just get this meeting over with."

> "I got a subtle flag in my spirit after I made that wisecrack," he admitted, "so I want to stick with the apology and ask your forgiveness here tonight."

For another example, Hybels writes, "At the start of an elders' meeting recently, one of Willow's elders began his prayer this way: 'God, may we have Your mind on the matters we're about to discuss.'"[3]

That's not an unusual prayer. What's unusual (in my opinion) is seeing a board or a leadership team who prays the prayer, then connects the dots to actually discern God's voice and live it out.

Referencing James 1:5 ("If any of you lacks wisdom…"), Hybels comments, "The challenge isn't whether or not He will send it [wisdom], but whether or not we will hear and heed it."

BOARDROOM LESSON

At the heart of Christ-centered governance is this core value: every board member will faithfully respond to the Holy Spirit's nudges and never exit a board meeting without addressing a relationship that is out of whack.

Board Action Steps:

○ **1. Read:** *The Power of a Whisper: Hearing God. Having the Guts to Respond.* by Bill Hybels.

○ **2. Reflect:** In assessing the health of our board member relationships, what question should our board chair ask at the close of every board meeting?

○ **3. Discuss:** If an outside observer evaluated our last board meeting, what would he or she describe as the defining characteristics and core values of our governance? Would they be Christ-centered?

Prayer: "Lord, help me to speak thoughtfully and cautiously. And when I don't, may grace abound. May we have Your mind on the matters we discuss. Amen."

PART 2:

BOARDROOM TOOLS, TEMPLATES, AND TYPOS

At least once every five years
every form should be put on trial for its life.[1]

Peter Drucker

4 | DO UNWRITTEN BOARD POLICIES REALLY EXIST?

Can't find that 10-year-old policy?
You need a BPM.

*Our attention to governance in general
and the BPM in particular revolutionized our board—
and I feel that I am the greatest beneficiary.
I am still on a honeymoon with the board after eight years![1]*

Rich Stearns, CEO at World Vision in 2006,
looking back on the development of their
Board Policies Manual (BPM).

Humor is a common commodity in effective board meetings, so when we mentioned at a board retreat that CEO succession planning should be a priority, the discussion prompted considerable laughter.

Boards need two kinds of plans: 1) An emergency executive transition plan, in case the CEO gets hit by the proverbial bus; and 2) A long-term succession plan, which is the ongoing, continuous process that boards implement (with the help of their CEOs).

That weekend, we noted that if the organization's CEO were to be hit by a bus and die, *we would all be sad for an appropriate amount of time*, but eventually the board would need to move forward and select the next leader.

Ironically, the board's governance committee had just completed—and proudly so—the first draft of the Board Policies Manual (BPM). A review of the BPM was on the agenda. Picking up on the bus discussion, the committee chair asked, "Would you recommend that we include in the Board Policies Manual a metric for the appropriate number of days we should be sad, should our CEO get hit by a bus?"

When the laughter died (pardon the pun), the question presented a wonderful teachable moment to discuss the practical and purposeful benefits of having a Board Policies Manual—a living document that collects all of the board's policies into one easy-to-find document of perhaps 20 pages or less.

If your board does not yet have a BPM, another board's experience may resonate with you: The ministry was formed more than 30 years before and there was no Board Policies Manual. Over those three decades, the ministry board had adopted dozens and dozens of policies. If all these policies were chronicled, it would reveal that every few years the board adopted conflicting policies covering the same topics—without even knowing there were existing policies. (Sad but true!)

Too many boards believe that written policies are unnecessary. After all, everyone knows the board policies—we record them in the board minutes. But watch what happens when a new member joins a board that relies on institutional memories or that presumes that the policy at any given time is whatever the board chair or the CEO says it is. This should not be justification to forego the benefits of a BPM.

Here's how one board dramatically improved their policy process. First, two board members raised the idea of developing a BPM. Unfortunately, the CEO did not champion the BPM project. Since this ministry had board term limits, every time that board made some progress on a BPM, there was turnover and the project languished.

Finally, the board formed a governance committee and the BPM project was assigned to the committee. After an 18-month effort, the board unanimously approved the first draft of the BPM, demonstrating their commitment to a new level of excellence.

Sadly, relatively few ministries have a BPM. As a result, these ministries lack the clarity in governance that the BPM provides.

There are several options and approaches for creating your BPM if you don't have one yet. We appreciate the simplicity and clarity of the BPM template featured in the book *Good Governance for Nonprofits: Developing Principles and Policies for an Effective Board* by Frederic L. Laughlin and Robert C. Andringa.[2]

While many organizations have written policies covering a wide range of topics, they're often filed away incoherently in the archives and no one can find them when needed. "Here's a fun job for a new board member," they say. "Please dig through 20 years of board minutes. Bring a flashlight and emergency provisions!"

There's a better way: the BPM. An effective BPM is usually under 20 pages and will address non-budgeted spending and dozens of other sticky policy issues. Plus, the BPM gives you a simple process for adding or revising policies at any board meeting.

Good Governance for Nonprofits is a practical "add water and stir" book and has everything, including a template for developing a BPM. Some committees arrive at their first draft after a full-day working session. (If you have several analytical types on the committee, it may take you longer—but the result will often be better!)

While a BPM project takes hard work and is time consuming, it is well worth the effort. It is as easy as three steps:

- **STEP 1: Commit to the concept.** Peter Drucker once said, "Plans are only good intentions unless they immediately degenerate into hard work."[3] A BPM will probably never be developed if it is just the CEO's idea; the board must get behind the project. Otherwise, the CEO will create a document that will never be properly utilized.

> *Good Governance for Nonprofits is a practical "add water and stir" book and has everything, including a template for developing a Board Policies Manual (BPM).*

Board members may feel that well-kept minutes are an acceptable substitute for a BPM. However, "meeting minutes are rarely written with the kind of specificity needed for well-constructed policies. . . . Archives of minutes are usually very inefficient libraries, and using them to research policies is often clumsy, inaccurate, and time-consuming."[4]

- **STEP 2: Develop the Board Policies Manual.** It may sound like a daunting task to develop a BPM, and this is where the project often dies. However, it can be broken down as follows:

  - ☑ Assign a coordinator. This could be the CEO, a board member, or a consultant.

  - ☑ Start with a template. The Word document version of the template from *Good Governance for Nonprofits* can be downloaded at: http://www.amacombooks.org/downloads/good-gov-nonprofits/

  - ☑ Fill in the template with known data.

  - ☑ Distribute the draft BPM to a review team.

  - ☑ Update and refine the BPM based on review team feedback.

  - ☑ Conduct a legal review of the revised BPM.

  - ☑ Present the BPM draft to the full board.

  - ☑ Begin operating with the approved BPM.

- **STEP 3. Integrate the Board Policies Manual.** Once the BPM is developed, you can now maximize this document to help you more effectively solve problems, make decisions, and build a stronger board. For example, here are three ways to use it:

☑ **Use the BPM to guide committee work.** If a committee recommends a new board policy or an amendment to an existing policy, the language of the resolution should be suitable for the appropriate section of the BPM. (Sometimes your governance committee will be designated to write the policy to ensure alignment.)

☑ **Use the BPM to guide board discussions.** Various questions may arise during the course of a board meeting that have already been addressed by the board. Simply refer to a policy in the BPM to resolve questions. Example: A board member wants to add an investment policy. The issue is resolved by pointing to an existing BPM policy adopted several years earlier.

The choice is yours: create and leverage an up-to-date BPM and improve your governance, or send out a search party for the last board member who trekked into the dusty archives.

When your BPM is a living document, you will include it with board materials for every board meeting and refer to it often. Then update it so it is consistent with every new policy adopted, and every revision of existing policies.

Once the BPM is implemented, you will never go back to your old ways!

BOARDROOM LESSON

Imagine the efficiency of having all your board policies in one document—a Board Policies Manual (BPM). Clearly this is a board best practice. Imagine onboarding new board members with a document that answers most of their questions. A BPM will help your board negotiate an emergency leadership transition, frame the strategic planning process, and give direction and boundaries in dozens of other important policy issues.

Board Action Steps:

○ 1. **Appoint:** Delegate the task of creating a Board Policies Manual to your governance committee or a special task force.

○ 2. **Read:** *Good Governance for Nonprofits: Developing Principles and Policies for an Effective Board* by Laughlin and Andringa, and download the BPM template.

○ 3. **Implement:** As Laughlin and Andringa suggest, keep the BPM available in all board meetings—so policy is current and clear—and integrate new board policies into the latest version of the BPM.

Prayer: "Lord, if creating a BPM will help us govern and steward more effectively—so our work is more eternity-oriented—then I'm available to serve on this project, with your help. Amen."

5 | *BEFORE* THE BOARD MEETING

Collaborate, then wisely build the board meeting agenda.

What should be the board's job outline?
It seems to me the best way to look at that question
is to see it through the prism of the agenda.[1]

Max De Pree

Few board members would question the importance of starting with a good agenda for a board meeting or board retreat. That is usually where the agreement ends. However, there are various ways the agenda can be established, depending on who develops the agenda and how the agenda is used in the meeting.

Consider Bill, who chairs a ministry board. When it comes to building the agenda, Bill believes this responsibility is totally his. He does ask the ministry CEO, Sarah, for any agenda additions. But Bill ultimately decides what is on the agenda, the sequence of the items, and the time allotted to each item. How does the CEO feel about this process? She likely feels excluded from the planning and wishes it was more collaborative.

Then there is Mary, who chairs another ministry board. She leaves every aspect of the agenda to Alan, the ministry's executive director. Mary doesn't even see the agenda until she arrives for the board meeting. Mary is not stepping up to her board chair responsibilities because she does not provide any input on the agenda.

Charles chairs yet another ministry board. He works closely with the ministry's CEO, Carol, to develop the board agenda, determine the optimal sequence of the agenda items and allocate time to each agenda item. Charles and Carol are confident that, through this participatory process, they have prepared an agenda that will effectively serve both the board and the ministry.

Regardless of who takes the lead in the agenda preparation, here are six significant principles:

1. **Create a high comfort level with the agenda.** When a board meeting agenda is finalized, both the board chair and the ministry's leader should have a high comfort level with the agenda. Otherwise, one or the other—or both—go into a board meeting with unnecessary anxiety.

2. **Allow for reconnection.** Relationships happen in the margin. Plan for adequate time for board members to reconnect with each other before delving into the agenda. Time for reconnection of board members increases in importance for boards that meet less frequently. This reconnecting could occur over a meal before the board meeting, or perhaps by sharing prayer requests followed by a time of prayer.

3. **Minimize minutiae.** One of the major tasks of a board agenda is to minimize minutiae. It is in the formation of the agenda allowing:

   ☐ perfunctory matters to be scheduled for routine treatment, perhaps many of them in a combined slot on the agenda.

   ☐ time for Q&A to handle any board follow-up for reports that were provided with the board materials, thus avoiding the need for each report to be "explained" to the board.

   ☐ time estimates to be assigned to each agenda item, which builds in a buffer to provide the board chair with flexibility when productive discussion goes longer than expected.

4. **Provide time for heavy lifting.** Many board agendas include one or more weighty issues. Generously allocate time on the agenda for these special issues. (For more on heavy lifting, see Lesson 36.)

   When the board chair and the CEO work together in building a sound board agenda, the board's process is significantly enhanced.

5. **Frame all actions.** *Always* frame potential board actions. How many times have you endured the pain of watching board members wordsmith a resolution from scratch?

   When board meeting materials are sent to the board in advance, the intent of every agenda item must be clear. There are usually three options: (1) inform, (2) accept,

(3) or approve. If approval of an item is sought, the proposed written resolution should be included. Of course, the board may change the wording of the proposed resolution, but the mere fact that the discussion starts with a carefully worded motion means that finishing the approval process is a much easier step. (See Lesson 19 for more information on framing board actions.)

6. **Allow adequate time for the executive session.** Too often, just 15 to 30 minutes is set aside for an executive session when an hour is needed. A rushed executive session is not productive for the board or the ministry's leader.

A truly exceptional board does not follow routine agendas or borrow another board's latest fad or formula. A truly exceptional board builds a governance structure and constructs a meeting agenda with serious intentionality and thus addresses the important and specific needs of its own unique organization.

God often works through processes as mundane as building the board agenda. Both the ministry's top leader and the board chair should bathe the agenda in prayer to allow the Holy Spirit to guide the board members during the meeting.

BOARDROOM LESSON

Preparing a quality board agenda is a prerequisite
for a quality board meeting.
A perfunctory board agenda destines the board
to a perfunctory board meeting.

Board Action Steps:

○ **1. Plan:** Begin preparing the board agenda at least several weeks in advance of the meeting.

○ **2. Collaborate:** The CEO and board chair should collaborate together in drafting the board agenda.

○ **3. Allocate:** Finalize the agenda, setting time allotments for each agenda item.

Prayer: "Lord, help us prepare a quality board agenda as the basis for an impactful board meeting. Amen."

6 | ELIMINATE HALLWAY WHINING

A 5/15 report to the board takes just five minutes to read and 15 minutes to write.

Individuals with written goals
were 39.5 percent more likely to succeed.
But there's more to the story.
Individuals who wrote their goals
and sent progress reports to friends
were 76.7 percent more likely to achieve them.[1]

Gary Keller with Jay Papasan

More than 20 years ago, a board chair suggested a simple—and fast—board reporting tool that changed my life and blessed the board. Today, hundreds of CEOs and boards are using this "*5/15 Report*" template.

Just days before writing this chapter, yet another CEO emailed his appreciation: "The *5/15 Reports* have been a home run. Thank you. We are now in full implementation mode on your recommendations."

Before we explain the *5/15 Report*, here's a pop quiz for board members and CEOs:

☑ CHECK: True or False?

T	F	Board Members
❏	❏	Informative reports to the board from our CEO are received regularly.
❏	❏	As a board member, I'm sometimes the last one to hear both good and bad news.
❏	❏	I receive way too many emails from our CEO, and I can't discern what's really important and what's really just an FYI.
❏	❏	I faithfully respond to every email or phone call from our CEO within 24 hours.
❏	❏	Our Board Policies Manual (BPM) establishes the type and frequency of CEO reports.

T	F	CEOs
❏	❏	I feel guilty that I'm not reporting adequately to the board in between meetings.
❏	❏	To be honest, I used to send more reports to the board, but no one ever read them.
❏	❏	I wish I felt more supported by the board. This is hard work. I don't think board members pray for me.
❏	❏	I have to keep the main thing the main thing: raising money. If I take time to write board reports that no one reads, it's a lose/lose.
❏	❏	Our Board Policies Manual (BPM) establishes the type and frequency of CEO reports.

In the hallways outside of boardrooms, perhaps the most constant whine is, "We don't hear anything from our CEO in between board meetings. How can I steward this ministry, if I'm not in the loop?"

CEOs also whine. "My board runs the continuum: the micro-managers want a weekly report. Others don't want email and they just call when they have a question. Frankly, I don't really bless anyone."

I was blessed one day when Pat Clements, my board chair at Christian Management Association (now Christian Leadership Alliance), introduced me to a simple, time-saving template. Like clock-work, on the fifteenth of every month, Clements, then CEO at Church Extension Plan, sent his *5/15 Report* to his national board. So I took his brilliant idea and customized it for the board of CMA and sent it out like clockwork on the 15th of every month. *The hallway whining stopped.*

> **CEO's MONTHLY *5/15 REPORT* TO THE BOARD**
> **5 Minutes to Read and 15 Minutes to Write**
> emailed on the 15th of every month

THE BIG IDEA. CEOs can write this report in just 15 minutes each month. Board members should be able to read it in just five minutes and enjoy a regular diet of good news, new news, and bad news. The content and frequency can be memorialized in the Board Policies Manual (BPM), by board action, so there is 100 percent board agreement on a report that serves the board's needs and expectations.

THE CONTENT. Customize the report so it meets your needs, but it will likely be five or fewer pages and easy to read when using a standard template. The content might include (in this order):

- Date/To/From/Subject

- Next Board Meeting: date, location, special details

- CEO's Monthly Dashboard Report on three to five board-approved annual SMART goals (Peter Drucker: "If you have more than five goals, you have none.")

  CEOs can write this report in just 15 minutes each month. Board members should be able to read it in just five minutes— and enjoy a regular diet of good news, new news, and bad news.

- Committee Highlights: bullet points only, and only if there is new information

- Board Nominating Committee "Pipeline Report": the running list of confidential prospect names under consideration

- Monthly Financial Report Summary: YTD vs. budget for revenue and expense

- Major Program Notes: bullet points

- Ministry Events Calendar & CEO's Travel Schedule: covers 12 to 24 months

- A Brief Ministry Story: a half-page maximum—for the board's encouragement

- Prayer Requests

- Personal Note from the CEO: one brief paragraph

- Board Meeting Schedule: covers the next 12 to 24 months, including dates, locations, times and two to four key agenda item bullet points for each meeting, such as audit, CEO annual review, budget approval, annual board self-assessment, etc.

After you have created and tested the first draft and received feedback from the board and the senior team, your *5/15 Report* template is ready to be systematized and delegated to the executive assistant or another team member. The template below may be a good starting point.

Point Person	Task	Dead-line	Date Done
Executive Assistant	Begin Draft #1: request reports from others	7th	
Senior Staff and Committee Chairs	Submit updates for report	10th	
CFO	Submit monthly financial report summary	12th	
Executive Assistant	Draft #2: All reports compiled	13th	
CEO	Dictate or approve "Ministry Story" and personal note; approve final draft	14th	
Executive Assistant	Email PDF of report to all board members (cc: senior team). Plus quarterly or occasionally, also email to selected former board members.	15th	

REMINDER #1: READERS OR LISTENERS? Not all board members are readers. Listening is the preferred learning style for some people. If possible, accommodate both styles. For your listeners, record the information, and email the recording, but keep it to five minutes or less.

REMINDER #2: THE FOUR SOCIAL STYLES. It's important for CEOs to communicate effectively for all four social styles:

- **The Analytical Style** appreciates communication that is clear and concise.

- **The Driving Style** prefers a "just stick to the facts" report.

- **The Amiable Style** says "get to know me;" content is often a lower priority.

- **The Expressive Style** wants you to listen to their opinions, so in your report ask for feedback and input.[2]

Not sure if the *5/15 Report* will work for your board? Test it for 90 days, then ask for feedback. We predict it will be a home run!

BOARDROOM LESSON

Establish a board policy on the content and frequency of CEO reports in between board meetings, then observe—the whining will stop!
Board members: respond to every *5/15 Report* with an encouraging email, note, or voicemail message within 24 hours. Your CEO's engagement will soar—as will accountability for achieving board-approved goals.

Board Action Steps:

○ 1. **Decide:** Assess the current status of between-meeting reports to the board and discern if a CEO's monthly *5/15 Report* to the board is worthy of a 90-day test period.

○ 2. **Delegate:** Inspire your CEO to delegate the gathering of information to the executive assistant or another staff person.

○ 3. **Respond:** Ask board members to respond to every monthly report with a quick email thanks, a note, or a voicemail message.

Prayer: "Lord, thank you for our CEO. Give our leader wisdom to know what to include in board reports. Give me discipline to read and respond on a timely basis. Amen."

7 | TYPOS MATTER!

"Pious shoddy is still shoddy."

*Amazon.com Inc. on Thursday blamed human error
for an outage at its cloud-services unit that caused widespread
disruption to internet traffic across the U.S. earlier this week.
In a post on its website, Amazon said
the outage started with a typo (bold added for emphasis)
at Amazon's northern Virginia data centers Tuesday.*[1]

The Wall Street Journal (March 2, 2017)

I peeked at my board chair's agenda page, and it was very unsettling. I couldn't believe it!

The day-long quarterly board meeting was about to start, and I was seated at the right hand of my board chair—a stellar human being, leader, and friend. His agenda, board recommendations, financial reports, and other materials were very neatly arranged in front of him, and he was paging through the board book and CEO reports I had prepared over numerous late-night marathons.

However, on almost every page, numerous words were circled. Normally, that would be a good thing. How blessed we were that our board chair had carefully read the materials in advance. How blessed we were that he even circled key words that he wanted to emphasize in the meeting.

Oops! Those circled words were—you guessed it—typos!

Oh, my. Graciously, my board chair said nothing about the typos that ricocheted across every page. He could have. Maybe he should have.

I learned a lesson in the boardroom that day. Murphy, of Murphy's Law fame, had already cautioned me:

Proofreading occurs best after publication.

True, the population seems to be divided into three groups:

- Group 1: Yikes! How did we miss that one?

- Group 2: Who Cares? With the ready response, "Get a life!"

- Group 3: Proofreaders who delight in detecting typos.

What about typos in your board reports, on your ministry's website, and in your donor letters? Do typos matter?

Imagine this scene (hypothetical, of course):

> You're seated in the exit row on a Boeing 747-400 at 30,000 feet. You're always anxious about flying, but somehow you have faith that the 147,000 pounds of high-strength aluminum, the 18 tires, and the 95,000-pound wings will get you from Los Angeles to London. After all, the 747 fleet has logged more than 35 billion

miles—enough to make 74,000 trips to the moon and back. A flight attendant mentions that it took 75,000 engineering drawings to produce the first 747.

While you're appreciating the extra leg room, you review the exit row emergency card, and your heart stops. There's not one, not two, but over a dozen typographical errors! Not minor ones—major errors. The airline would be embarrassed with the careless proofreading.

A cold shiver comes next. Wait a minute. If the proofreading is shoddy, what about the safety precautions? Should I drink the water? Who serviced the engines? Is there enough fuel? Maybe the fuel guy left early for lunch and forgot to fill all the tanks. Who's in charge of pilot training, the same guy who hires the proofreaders?[2]

Proofreading matters. When your board members, customers, members, givers, and volunteers see typos and mediocre materials, it matters. Theologian Elton Trueblood said it best:

Pious shoddy is still shoddy.

After that embarrassing board meeting, I asked around. I learned that every publication, from *The Wall Street Journal* to a one-page bi-monthly enewsletter, must follow a stylebook and have its own style sheet. A stylebook will enable your entire team to follow a consistent set of writing rules. Board reports, of course, are no exception; they must be well-written. As Fred Smith, Sr., said, "I learned to write to burn the fuzz off my thinking."[3]

I also learned that more than two million journalists own the *Associated Press (AP) Stylebook and Briefing on Media Law*, the bible for journalists. This invaluable resource includes more than 5,000 entries on grammar, spelling, punctuation (there is no period in Dr Pepper), capitalization, abbreviations (Calif., not CA), misused words ("Canadian geese" are more correctly referred to as Canada geese) and the correct names of countries, organizations, Arabic words, and brand names.

> *A cold shiver comes next. Wait a minute. If the proofreading is shoddy, what about the safety precautions?*

For this book, *Lessons From the Nonprofit Boardroom*, our copy editor followed *The Chicago Manual of Style*[4], but with some exceptions when we used our own stylesheet.

For the punctuation and proofreading zealots on your board and team, buy them the bestseller *Eats, Shoots & Leaves: The Zero Tolerance Approach to Punctuation* by Lynne Truss. The author dedicates the book "to the memory of the striking Bolshevik printers of St. Petersburg who, in 1905, demanded to be paid the same rate for punctuation marks as for letters, and thereby directly precipitated the first Russian Revolution."[5]

We can chuckle because we've all made our fair share of typos. Yet, high standards of proofreading coupled with well-written and well-proofed board agendas and reports will enhance the effectiveness of your ministry.

Note this powerful reminder, often attributed to John Wesley: "Our responsibility is to give the world the right impression of God." Well-proofed board materials will help you do that!

BOARDROOM LESSON

The care and preparation you put into written board agendas, reports, and recommendations represent a deeper context: the care and thoughtfulness expected throughout the ministry. Well-written reports (with a typo-free goal) also speak to an even deeper conviction. We desire "to give the world the right impression of God."

Board Action Steps:

○ 1. **Delegate:** If you have board members who write board reports, minutes, and other documents, but who are not effective proofreaders, build in adequate turn-around time, so proofreading can be delegated to others.

○ 2. **Enhance Consistency:** Ask your CEO to delegate the writing of your organization's "style sheet" to an appropriate person, then enhance your board reports with a consistent style for spelling, punctuation, capitalization, and other editing rules.

Prayer: "Lord, thank you for publishers who give us your Holy Bible without typos! Likewise, with our board reports, we want to give everyone the right impression of you. So thank you for our proofreaders, and help us to be gracious when we do spot those pesky typos! Amen."

PART 3

NOMINEES FOR THE BOARD MEMBER HALL OF FAME

Make this your common practice:
Confess your sins to each other and pray for each other
so that you can live together whole and healed.
The prayer of a person living right with God is something
powerful to be reckoned with.

Elijah, for instance, human just like us,
prayed hard that it wouldn't rain, and it didn't—
not a drop for three and a half years.
Then he prayed that it would rain, and it did.
The showers came and everything started growing again.

James 5:16-18 (MSG)

8 | LISTEN TO THE WISDOM OF MANY COUNSELORS

Don't ask board members to vote against God!

> *By your grace, my leadership will either enhance or restrain*
> *the work of your Spirit in those who lead me, making them*
> *more effective or less effective. Those I choose to follow*
> *will have a profound impact on the results in the organization,*
> *and they will have a profound impact on me.*[1]
>
> Richard Kriegbaum

As we've reflected over what we've learned and observed from hundreds and hundreds of boardroom experiences, there's a common discipline that is all too uncommon: LISTENING!

At one memorable breakfast, I had a zillion questions for Frank (not his real name), a seasoned CEO, and yet he was amazingly patient with my naïveté.

"So, Frank," I asked this savvy leader, "how do you walk that tightrope of leading the ministry without usurping or minimizing the board's role?"

He thanked our server—by name—for a second cup of coffee. (*Oh, good,* I thought, *he still has time for more questions.*) Then he shared this story.

"It's a delicate dance. Yes, the board wants you to lead, but it's their job to define the parameters."

John Carver's Policy Governance® model describes this as the corral. The board must agree where the fences are. Based on leadership competencies, resources, risks, and many other factors, the board is able to regularly move the fences in or out with the crystal-clear understanding that the CEO and staff have board-approved authority to operate inside the corral, but not outside. Many boards function with a Board Policies Manual that delineates the corral boundaries. (See Lesson 4.)

"Just do it and don't ask the board for any input—because I don't want to fly all the way from Dallas to Chicago just to vote against God!"

Frank continued, "I thought I did this pretty well, and the board was basically happy with my leadership. But then during a coffee break at a quarterly board meeting, one of my favorite board members pulled me aside.

"He began, 'Frank, I have some angst about your report and recommendations. Don't misunderstand. I appreciate you and your leadership. But all morning, you used a troubling phrase with our board:

> **'God told me** we should launch this program.'
> **'God told me** we should move into this region.'
> **'God told me** we should budget for this new initiative.'

'So if you plan to continue to tell your board that "God told me," and if you're absolutely sure God told you to do something, just do it.

'Just do it and don't ask the board for any input because I don't want to fly all the way from Dallas to Chicago just to vote against God!

'However, if you believe—like I do—that the Scriptures teach there is wisdom in many counselors, then please edit your rhetoric so we can discuss, discern, and decide based on the combined wisdom of our board, not just your wisdom!'"

Oh, my. Frank's transparency was stunning. He laughed about it—in a confessional way—and he admitted it changed the trajectory of his leadership.

If there actually was a Board Member Hall of Fame, a picture of Frank's board member would be displayed in a prominent location.

BOARDROOM LESSON

Edit your leadership rhetoric so all board members are encouraged to share their insights and discernment. Avoid pronouncements that begin with "God told me!"

Listen. Listen. Listen.

Board Action Steps:

○ 1. **Read:** Ask a board member to read and report on *Pursuing God's Will Together: A Discernment Practice for Leadership Groups* by Ruth Haley Barton, especially Chapter 11, with 10 listening guidelines.

○ 2. **Evaluate:** At your next end-of-meeting evaluation, ask an observer to comment on the listening skills of the board. Ask this person to note examples when the board sought to hear from God and if any inappropriate rhetoric tainted the discussion.

○ 3. **View:** Frame this scripture for your boardroom wall: "Plans fail for lack of counsel, but with many advisers they succeed." (Proverbs 15:22, NIV)

Prayer: "Lord, teach me to be a better listener and to thirst for wisdom. Amen."

9 | SERVE WITH HUMILITY AND EXPERIENCE GOD'S PRESENCE

One board chair creates a holy moment for his CEO search committee.

> *Humility is the only soil in which the graces take root;*
> *the lack of humility is the sufficient explanation*
> *of every defect and failure.*[1]
>
> Andrew Murray

When Jeff Lilley completed his application for the president/CEO position at Seattle's Union Gospel Mission, he stopped to pray and reflect on this question:

> You're preparing for your first meeting as President, with your seven direct reports at the Mission. What are some of the key things you'll share with them? And, list two or three books you'd like them to read and why.

Jeff recommended the book *Humility* by Andrew Murray (just 59 pages). He wrote:

> This is a dangerous book. But I believe God is constantly seeking for the humble who will surrender their will and life to Him. If a ministry is successful and effective, it is because the Lord is guiding that ministry. The Christian community has some strained

views on humility, and we often live with a false humility that sometimes hinders our effectiveness. In addition, we have seen that the very success of our ministry sometimes creates a sense of arrogance, and this book addresses that issue well.

So—and this may surprise you—we're not nominating Jeff Lilley to the Board Member Hall of Fame, we're nominating two of his former board chairs! (See Lesson 10 for the second nominee.)

Andy Toles, a Seattle attorney, was the board chair who, with the search committee, prayed and discerned for direction in the selection of the next leader for Seattle's Union Gospel Mission. After extensive deliberation and due diligence, the committee selected Jeff Lilley. A year later, when the four committee members met to conduct Jeff's annual performance review, one committee member interrupted with this:

> *"I will go to my grave remembering that holy moment as one of the top spiritual experiences of my life."*

> Before we start, I just want to remind us all to think back a year ago, when we were interviewing the final three candidates, including Jeff, and God met us in that interview room. I will go to my grave remembering that holy moment as one of the top spiritual experiences of my life.

Some board chairs favor delegation instead of discernment. Not Andy Toles. Not only did this board chair lead an extraordinarily effective search process that resulted in a new ministry leader, but God also used him as the catalyst for a defining God moment in the life of a fellow board member.

Hence, we nominate Andy Toles to the Board Member Hall of Fame!

Toles is representative, of course, of thousands and thousands of board chairs and board members across the nation who serve humbly, faithfully, and with joy. God blesses leaders with character. As General Norman Schwarzkopf once noted, "Leaders need two things—character and strategy. If you can do only one, drop strategy."[2]

While there is no actual Board Member Hall of Fame (to our knowledge), we do encourage boards to celebrate excellence in the boardroom and to affirm board members for their faithfulness and fruitfulness.

Who would you nominate to the Board Member Hall of Fame?

BOARDROOM LESSON

In the busyness of board work, invite God's presence
to permeate your agenda, your decisions, and your
relationships. You'll be creating the space for holy moments—
those times in our earthly service when board members
are listening and Heaven speaks.
Treasure those times.

Board Action Steps:

○ 1. **Share:** Give copies of *Humility*, by Andrew Murray, to
each board member.

○ 2. **Discuss:** Humble, hungry, and smart (people smart)
are the critical virtues for a team, says Patrick Lencioni
in *The Ideal Team Player: How to Recognize and
Cultivate the Three Essential Virtues.*[3] Would others
affirm that your board leads with humility?

○ 3. **Nominate:** As a boardroom exercise, team up in groups
of two and invest seven minutes in discussing what
might be the criteria for your board's nominee to the
Board Member Hall of Fame.

Prayer: "Lord, none of us serve on this board with fame in
view. Like John Wesley, we desire to 'judge all things only by
the price they shall gain in eternity.' Amen."

10 | PRIORITIZE PRAYER OVER PROBLEMS

Create space for prayer—serious supplications for a serious work.

> *...And dear God, help us to remain unified. Help us to remember*
> *that few decisions are worth the divisions caused by*
> *dominant winning or belligerent losing.*
> *Help us to seek your glory and not ours.*
> *Grant us the joy of arriving at adjournment closer to one another*
> *because we are closer to you.*[1]
>
> Dan Bolin

"Where's the prayer?"

The quarterly board meeting at Seattle's Union Gospel Mission was about to start, and that was the question that Linda Ranz, the board chair, asked Jeff Lilley, the president/CEO.

Linda: Jeff, where's the board prayer?

Jeff: What board prayer?

Linda: You know. It's titled "A Board Prayer," and we read it at the last meeting. You gave copies to every board member, and we went around the board table several times, each of us reading a sentence out loud. It was powerful! So where are those copies?

Jeff was confused but enjoying every moment. Of all the issues facing the board at this meeting, his board chair was hyper-focused on prayer!

Jeff: Well, since we read the prayer at the last meeting, I didn't bring copies for this meeting.

Linda: Don't you remember? It was so powerful and such a great preamble for doing God's work here, that we agreed to read the prayer at every board meeting!

Jeff: I'll get the prayer— and I'll be right back!

So they read "A Board Prayer" and were reminded, once again, that issues like reporting, mission clarity, listening, speaking, planning, and unity all require inviting the God of the Universe into the work and relationships of the board.

Not content to begin God's work with "three points and a poem" or a clever devotional off the internet, this board chair created a boardroom culture that prioritized prayer over problems.

That year, Jeff and several board members participated in a board leadership and development program hosted by a foundation that equips board members to be more effective stewards. The program encourages boards to use "A Board Prayer" as a helpful tool during their meetings. Written by Dan Bolin, the two-page prayer is now used by hundreds of boards around the world. (Your board can also read the prayer, or portions of it, at every board meeting. See Lesson 40 for the complete prayer.)

Linda Ranz understood ministry priorities. Not content to begin God's work with "three points and a poem" or a clever devotional off the internet, this board chair created a boardroom culture that prioritized prayer over problems.

Hence, in addition to nominating her board chair predecessor, Andy Toles (see Lesson 9), to the Board Member Hall of Fame, we are also nominating Linda Ranz.

Linda Ranz is also representative, of course, of board chairs and board members in thousands of ministries who believe that Christ-centered governance has a boardroom distinctive that requires the right theology and serious intentionality about prayer.

John Pellowe notes that a board's theology is key. He quotes Charles Olsen, who says that

> the board of a Christian organization is the people of God in community. The group is the body of Christ, with members having varying gifts, wisdom, and functions. As such the group's life is formed by scripture, prayer, silent waiting, witnessing, and serving. . . . The meeting will no longer be seen as a gathering of individual people with business to transact, but as the functioning of the body [of Christ].[2]

Pellowe adds, "This [inspiring theological statement by Charles Olsen] is so profound that I feel every Christian board would benefit from reading it at the beginning of every meeting."[3]

Before you begin every board meeting, discern what you might read or pray together to invite God's holy presence to permeate your agenda, your decisions, and your relationships.

BOARDROOM LESSON

When you take time to pray—not perfunctory "bless us" prayers but prayers with power and faith—God promises to hear and act. Encourage your board chair to make space for prayer, for quiet, and for discerning God's voice.

Board Action Steps:

○ 1. **Pray:** At the beginning, at the end, and frequently during your board meetings, pray!

○ 2. **Affirm:** Encourage your board chair to leave ample agenda time for planned and unplanned prayer.

○ 3. **Read:** Distribute copies of "A Board Prayer" and, going around the room until the prayer is completed, ask each board member to read one bullet point. Then in groups of two, ask each person to share one or more points that hit home.

Prayer: "Lord, we pray—along with Dan Bolin—'Help us to see the issues before us from many perspectives—but ultimately from your perspective. Align our thoughts with your thoughts and our work with your desire.' Amen."

PART 4:

EPIPHANIES
IN THE
BOARDROOM

Why are you doing what others can do,
when you are leaving undone what only you can do?[1]

11 | *TAP! TAP! TAP!*

When the Spirit nudges your board, does
He hear a busy signal?

> *If we are to engage in meaningful spiritual discernment with others,*
> *and listen well for His will for our shared ministry life,*
> *we first need to tend to the state of our own hearts.*[1]
>
> Stephen A. Macchia

Your board meetings probably always open and close with
prayer. Some of your board members would certainly
consider anything less to be sacrilege!

What about between the opening and closing bell at your
board meetings? Does your board send up prayers at
appropriate times? Is your board meeting ever interrupted by
the spontaneous singing of the Doxology?

Now, the review of the minutes from the last board meeting
may not require prayer. Neither am I suggesting that boards
should routinely pray for most board agenda items. This
could reduce prayer to a perfunctory level.

But investing time in prayer should not be limited to those
challenging fork-in-the-road board decisions. Share prayers

of thanksgiving to celebrate God's hand in achieving a significant goal.

The arms of your CEO may be weary. Pray after your board hears the CEO's report or when you sense the load is heavy. Remember in Exodus 17:12 how Aaron and Hur held up Moses's hands, one on each side. "So his hands remained steady until sunset." A prayer of encouragement can have a similar effect for your CEO.

Based on my many years of board service, it is my observation that boards often miss prime opportunities to be empowered by our Heavenly Father. It's this simple: God's power is revealed in the boardroom when board members pray together.

God wants to release His power in your boardroom. This power may come in the form of:

- **Wisdom**—a plan of action that the board cannot determine on its own.

- **Courage**—more than the board could ever muster on its own.

- **Confidence**—uncommon belief that the board is on the right track.

- **A Miracle**—for example: when God moves a giver to fill a huge financial need.

Our colleague Stephen A. Macchia explains the nudge of the Holy Spirit as the *"Tap! Tap! Tap!"* of the Spirit on our hearts.[2]

How can your board avoid missing that nudge from the Holy Spirit? Let me share a few ways:

- **Realize we need God's help.** God's power comes when boards realize they cannot handle things on their own. Boards must enter the boardroom with a receptivity to hearing from the Holy Spirit. This attitude is the opposite of asserting that we have all the answers in and of ourselves. *Tap! Tap! Tap!*

- **Develop the discipline of stillness.** Too often, boards do not seize opportunities to be still. They do not become quiet and mindfully listen for His voice. Times of stillness and solitude were important to Jesus (Mark 1:35). The Apostle Peter went up on the roof to pray at lunchtime, and God talked to him there (Acts 10:9-20). Scripture is filled with people who took time to hear what God had to say to them. *Tap! Tap! Tap!*

  > *It is possible to be aware of God's gentle promptings throughout the board meeting and still efficiently complete the agenda.* Tap! Tap! Tap!

- **Commit to slow down—lower the RPMs.** If the board is typically running behind on its agenda and the pace of the meeting is moving too quickly, it may seem like taking time to pray for key decisions imposes on the meeting schedule. It is possible to be aware of God's gentle promptings throughout the board meeting and still efficiently complete the agenda. *Tap! Tap! Tap!*

- **Understand that any board member can feel the nudge of the Holy Spirit.** It may seem as if only the board chair should call for prayer during the meeting. Not so—every board member has equal access to the Holy Spirit hotline. The board chair should make it clear that all members should feel free to "throw the flag" when they sense that it is time for prayer. *Tap! Tap! Tap!*

When a board prays regularly, sincerely, and specifically during board meetings, God will answer these prayers and He will be glorified.

To go deeper in this area, consider how St. Ignatius identified three distinct times when faced with making Spirit-filled choices:

1. **A revelatory time**—beyond a shadow of a doubt, the conviction is crystal clear (Saul fell to the ground, blinded by the light).

2. **A discerning time**—facing big decisions, interior movements of consolation or desolation pull you toward or push you away from a decision.[3]

3. **A waiting time**—like a sailboat without any wind, there is no strong consolation or desolation.

A revelatory time may not require prayer during a board meeting. But when a board is in a discerning or a waiting time, prayer is often just what a board needs.

BOARDROOM LESSON

When the Spirit nudges your board,
does He hear a busy signal?
All board members should be attentive
to the nudges of the Holy Spirit, throwing the prayer flag
when prompted on behalf of the entire board.

Board Action Steps:

○ 1. **Read:** Ask one or more board members to read (and report on) Ruth Haley Barton's book *Pursuing God's Will Together*.[4]

○ 2. **Review:** Reflect on your recent board meetings. Were there times when the board should have stopped to pray but did not?

○ 3. **Listen:** Be alert for those *Tap! Tap! Tap!* moments in board meetings. Then stop and pray.

Prayer: "Lord, nudge our board when you want us to stop—even in the middle of a board meeting—and ask for your guidance. Amen."

12 | VISION GROWTH MUST EQUAL LEADER GROWTH

Caution! Vision-casting often backfires.

If the board and the CEO have lasting substantive differences, they have a choice: stay with the strategy or replace the CEO. Consider that management has a shelf life too, just like the strategy.[1]

Ram Charan

It seemed like a good idea at the time.

I was the very young executive director of a Christian camp and conference center in the Northwest. Its rich ministry history was remarkable given the postage stamp-size property—just ten acres.

It was my first CEO role, and my board was both encouraging and forgiving. But board meetings tended to focus on budgets, buildings, and banquets (the fundraising type). So I asked several mentors how I could raise the vision of the board.

"Schedule a vision-casting trip," was the common wisdom.

So I did. We scheduled a board retreat at Warm Beach Camp and Conference Center, the largest and most effective camping ministry in Washington. I asked Bob McDowell, the camp's visionary leader, to facilitate the weekend, inspire our board, and give us a tour of the property (which was huge, in our eyes).

Bob was so gracious and amazingly gifted. His talks were extraordinary. His vision for ministry—stunning. His unique gifting impressed: pastor, pilot, pianist, prophet, and people person.

And boy, did he raise the vision quotient of our board members!

Our board retreat included spouses, so on Saturday afternoon, Bob piled all of us onto the camp bus (they had their own bus!) for a tour of all 278 acres. His transparency was vivid. "We built those buildings a few years ago, but we made some mistakes. Learn from our lessons."

Bob drove as he narrated the history and long range plans of this very special ministry, now with more than 600 beds. He shared, what today we would label, a "Big Holy Audacious Goal"—and none of us doubted that the plans would be realized.

Oh, my. This imaginative leader, with a bold faith and a humble heart, was just what our board needed. (Little did I know.)

My wife, Joanne, overheard a board member's wife whisper to her husband, "Where do you think we could get an executive director like Bob?"

Joanne was only slightly offended, and to her credit shared that observation only with me. I laughed, not really worried about my tenure. Years later, though, I understood the lesson that I should have learned that day—and the lesson that all boards must learn: Do we have the right CEO leading us for this unique season of ministry? As stewards of the ministry ("stewards of a sacred trust," as David McKenna pronounces this holy duty[2]), board members must keep this big question on the front burner.

Ram Charan notes the two most important issues that boards must continuously address: "There is nothing more important for a CEO than having the right strategy and right choice of goals, and for the board, the right strategy is second only to having the right CEO."[3]

During my years at Willow Creek Community Church and Willow Creek Association, I heard Bill Hybels frequently urge the large church staff to "hold your jobs loosely." With palms open to God's leading and board or senior leaders' discernment, Bill urged each of us to unclasp our too-tight grips on our titles, positions, and in-the-spotlight roles.

Sometimes growth overwhelms leaders. We can handle 1X size of ministry and responsibilities, but not 3X. "Hold your job loosely."

> *With palms open to God's leading and board or senior leaders' discernment, Bill urged each of us to unclasp our too-tight grips on our titles, positions, and in-the-spotlight roles.*

Boards must be equally discerning when recruiting and selecting a CEO as they are when determining if it is time for their current CEO to exit. It's often the most difficult decision a board will face—but they must. Many times only a new CEO with fresh thinking and fresh energy will bring new passion and perhaps needed gifting for your organization's next season of ministry.

BOARDROOM LESSON

When you inspire your board to elevate its vision, sometimes that vision may require an exit plan for the CEO who is unable to deliver on that vision. But that's okay.

Board Action Steps:

○ 1. **Read:** Discuss the questions in *Owning Up: The 14 Questions Every Board Member Needs to Ask* at your next board retreat, or select one or two questions per board meeting during your "10 Minutes for Governance" segment (see Lesson 39).

○ 2. **Vision-cast:** Hold your next board meeting or board retreat at a ministry location that will inspire the board to think courageously about the future.

○ 3. **Pray:** "Oh, Lord, give me faith for this leap to the future. And make this a leap of leadership, not a solo jump."[4]

Prayer: "Lord, give our board wisdom and discernment as we encourage and support our ministry's CEO. And give us courage to address early on those specific areas where our leader needs to grow. Amen."

13 | IF YOU NEED A VOLUNTEER, RECRUIT A VOLUNTEER

If you need a board member, recruit a board member.

If you chase two rabbits . . . you will not catch either one.[1]

Russian Proverb

It was Saturday morning of the overnight board retreat at a Minnesota camp and time for a coffee break. I was feeling pretty good. The PowerPoint worked. The executive director had inspired the full board to attend, and they were friendly to this out-of-state leader.

Energized with caffeine, we resumed the board enrichment sessions until I noticed an empty chair. I paused, "Should we wait for Hank?"

Silence. Then muffled chuckles filled the room. So I asked, "What's so funny?"

No one offered to snitch on Hank, so I resumed my driver-mode, too-much-content road show until a noisy power saw in the next building interrupted my monologue.

More laughter. Not muffled.

"Here's the deal," I demanded with a phony sternness. "Either you tell me what's so funny, or I'm packing up the PowerPoint!"

Finally, the board chair intervened. "So sorry! Really, we do appreciate all of this board stuff. But Hank is our buildings and grounds committee chair, and it's his job to get that cabin remodeled before summer. He told me he'd prefer completing his construction work today rather than wasting his time—I mean, investing his time in this board training session. I'm sure you understand."

Yikes! That was a punch in the gut. But fortunately, before that emotion spilled out my mouth, the Lord gave me a gentle nudge that was paradigm changing. In that moment in Minnesota, I had a profound epiphany.

> *Hank's joy meter always ramped up when he mixed sawdust with service.*

These God-honoring men and women had recruited Hank onto the camp board and the buildings and grounds committee with righteous motives, but for all the wrong reasons. Sure, he owned a power saw and his own construction company, but for Hank, sitting in a boring board meeting was a major irritant. (Actually, as a construction guy, he used a few other words.)

Hank's heart resonated with Eric Liddell, the Scottish runner in the 1924 Olympics, who said, "I believe God made me for a purpose . . . but he also made me fast. And when I run, I feel His pleasure."[2] Hank's joy meter always ramped up when he mixed sawdust with service.

So that morning, we talked about Hank, board service, and joy at that fork-in-the-road board retreat. We talked about balancing board roles by defining the three board hats: the Governance Hat, the Volunteer Hat, and the Participant Hat.

This insight was birthed that weekend:

**If you need a board member, recruit a board member.
If you need a volunteer, recruit a volunteer.**

Peter Drucker, the father of modern management and a champion of nonprofit organizations, once said, "There is one thing all boards have in common. . . . *They do not function.*"[3]

You may chuckle at Drucker's tongue-in-cheek wisdom, but was he describing your board? By understanding these three hats—three distinct board roles—you will eliminate confusion and dysfunction for your current board. When interviewing prospective board members, you can clearly articulate these core principles so new board members will avoid bringing their own delightful dysfunctions into your boardroom.

The best boards carefully delineate the Volunteer Hat from the Governance Hat by affirming these two principles:

❑ **PRINCIPLE 1: Many can volunteer, but only the board can govern.** Bruce Bugbee, author of *What You Do Best in the Body of Christ*, said a friend once asked him, "Why are you doing what others can do when you are leaving undone what only you can do?"[4]

Board members are directly accountable to God for the ministry. To spiritually discern God's direction takes time.

Only the board can set direction, establish and revise policies, select and support the CEO, and monitor and measure results.

So with God's leading, boards must recruit competent men and women for board service, especially those who have passion for good governance. And good governance takes time and often leaves little or no time for other volunteer roles.

❑ **PRINCIPLE 2: Volunteering is optional.** Volunteer service must be passion-based and aligned with a volunteer's spiritual gifts and strengths. At the end of every board meeting, the CEO might say:

> "Just a reminder that we need 50 key volunteers this year. If you have the passion, spiritual gifting, and strengths to tackle a volunteer project, then let's talk. Of course, your volunteer role is separate from your governance role—and every board member need not be a volunteer. But if you do volunteer, please remove your Governance Hat when wearing your Volunteer Hat!"

BOARDROOM LESSON

Not all volunteers are competent as board members.
So as you recruit board members, find men and women
who understand—and are effective at wearing—the
Governance Hat. Governance includes: God-honoring
discernment (as a group), stewarding and sustaining the
ministry, measuring and monitoring programs,
focusing on the future, hiring/firing the CEO, and much
more. That takes time—and special expertise.

Board Action Steps:

○ 1. **View and Engage:** As a board, watch the short video in
the *ECFA Governance Toolbox Series No. 2: Balancing
Board Roles—Understanding the 3 Board Hats:
Governance, Volunteer, Participant.*[5]

○ 2. **True or False?** At least annually, we review our board's
committee structure to ensure that our committees are
focused on governance work, not on staff or volunteer
work.

○ 3. **Assess:** Are there individuals on our board we could
bless by releasing them to their greater passions—their
volunteer roles?

Prayer: "Lord, give us discernment to identify future board
members who love and are enriched by the governance role,
and lead us to equally competent people who find joy in using
their gifts in volunteer roles. Amen."

14 | IF YOU NEED A BOARD MEMBER, RECRUIT A BOARD MEMBER

If you need a volunteer, recruit a volunteer.

> *Policy development is not an occasional board chore but its chief occupation.*[1]
>
> John Carver

Several years ago, the trustees for a regional foundation had a defining moment in a board meeting. Every quarter as they prayed for discernment when approving grant awards, they kept asking, "How could we foster further effectiveness through our grant-making?"

Then this epiphany!

> What if we inspired the board members of our grantees to be more effective? If nonprofit ministry boards were more effective, wouldn't they be more effective stewards of our grants? And with stronger and more highly engaged boards—would not the ministries see more Kingdom impact?

With that mustard seed of an idea, the foundation trustees funded a leadership program for board members. Amazingly, that one board decision—prompted by an effectiveness inquiry—launched a ripple effect of healthy boards throughout the region.

Now fast forward. I'm the board coach for a ministry participating in the leadership program. My coaching assignment was to facilitate a board enrichment session, but the board chair also needed a few minutes for board business. I was grateful, because board coaches can learn much by observing a board meeting, even a brief one.

I was skeptical. Would this robust ministry that frequently said yes to every new opportunity in their needy niche have the discipline to recruit people to the board who had passion for governance, which often means saying no? Or, as Ralph E. Enlow, Jr., cautions, "Good planning is not the accumulation of everyone's aspirations. Ultimately, a plan represents the *elimination* of options."[2]

Or, like so many boards, would the boardroom be half-empty with people who loved their volunteer roles but frankly were clueless about the Governance Hat?

And why does this matter—recruiting people who are competent in governance?

Our collective misunderstanding about governance roles and responsibilities is ironic. We expect restaurants to have competent chefs. We trust airline pilots to be trained up to the minute and highly competent. We expect theologians to be lifelong learners as they "rightly divide the Word." Yet, board members, not so much.

Would this ministry, I wondered, have that "warm body to fill a slot" mindset about board recruitment, or perhaps an inappropriate job description for their board members?

According to John Carver, who is widely regarded as the guru of Policy Governance®, the chief occupation of the board is the development of policy. For Christ-centered boards, this means board members invest the bulk of their time in chewing, praying, discerning, and making God-honoring decisions.

"Governing by policy," writes Carver, "means governing out of policy in the sense that no board activity takes place without reference to policies. Most resolutions in board meetings will be motions to amend the policy structure in some way. *Consequently, policy development is not an occasional board chore but its chief occupation.*" [3]

There were no raised eyebrows or rolling eyes. No "this is boring, let's get to the fun stuff" whining. They engaged. They were thoughtful. And they were good at their governance jobs— competent people doing competent board work.

So as this ministry's coach, I was blessed to observe that the foundation's investment in training was already reaping a dividend in this boardroom! The CEO, who was well-known in the community, asked the board's counsel on whether or not to accept an invitation to a local politician's reception (and fundraiser).

I watched as the board members (two college profs, a county executive, a business leader, an influential pastor, an entrepreneur, and others) wrestled with the issue and wordsmithed a succinct policy that would govern the organization's path through the grey areas of governance in the trenches.

There were no raised eyebrows or rolling eyes. No "this is boring, let's get to the fun stuff" whining. They engaged. They were thoughtful. And they were good at their governance jobs—competent people doing competent board work.

When it was my turn to facilitate the board enrichment segment, I delivered verbal high-fives and affirmed them for their God-honoring discernment. They understood that in board meetings, their chief occupation was to wear their Governance Hats, not their Volunteer Hats.

Imagine! One foundation board with one agenda item— greater effectiveness—launched a ripple effect of healthy governance.

Watch for the next book in this series, *More Lessons From the Nonprofit Boardroom*, with commentary on the Participant Hat, and how to use an annual board member annual affirmation template.

BOARDROOM LESSON

Avoid airlines that employ rookie pilots who have passion for aeronautics, but no experience or competence. Likewise, ensure that you are crystal clear about the roles and responsibilities of board members and recruit men and women who have already demonstrated competence in God-honoring governance.

Board Action Steps:

○ 1. **View:** At your next nominating or governance committee meeting, walk the group through the viewing guide checklists in the *ECFA Governance Toolbox Series No. 1: Recruiting Board Members.*[4]

○ 2. **Review:** Discuss the 10 basic responsibilities of nonprofit boards[5] from BoardSource, and consider what additional responsibilities should be added for Christ-centered boards.

○ 3. **Delegate:** Inspire a board member to help increase the board's competencies in policy development by reading a book, booklet, or article on Policy Governance®, the term coined by John Carver.[6]

Prayer: "Lord, continue to guide us toward men and women who are competent in governance and experience joy in establishing God-honoring policy. Amen."

PART 5:

BOARDROOM BLOOPERS

A greeter at Walmart gets more orientation
than most board members ever do.[1]

Patrick Lencioni

15 | CUT YOUR LOSSES

Is it a $30,000 baseball or not?

> *The more you prepare for the meeting before the meeting,*
> *the less time you will have to spend doing damage control after*
> *the meeting. A leader never has to recover from a good start.*[1]
>
> John Maxwell

In my spare time, I am a baseball researcher and collector of memorabilia. Normal folks might enjoy a few hours walking through the Baseball Hall of Fame Museum and Library in Cooperstown, NY. Abnormal people—like me—enjoy spending several days at a stretch conducting research in the library.

There are a number of sports collectors' conventions regularly held around the country. I drop by one or two of these each year just to keep up with what is happening in the world of vintage baseball collectibles.

In King of Prussia, PA, I was walking around the floor of a collector's convention with a friend who is also a CPA, though neither of us are now actively practicing accounting. We paused to look at some items at one booth.

The dealer recognized us and knew we were CPAs. He said, "I apologize for asking you a professional question, but I need help with a tax issue."

The dealer said he had bought a baseball earlier in the year and was convinced that it had been autographed by the great New York Yankee home run slugger Babe Ruth. He paid $30,000 for the baseball. While this is a lot of money, a pristine ball cleanly autographed by the Babe on the "sweet spot" carries a very high value.

He said that he had the ball examined by several groups that authenticate sports memorabilia. In each case, the verdict came back—the signature was a fake. The baseball had absolutely no value.

My CPA friend and I explained how the owner of a baseball with a fake signature could document and claim his loss for tax purposes. We were careful to share with him that our advice might be worth what it cost him, and we walked on.

Reflecting on the discussion with the dealer about his worthless baseball, I was reminded that occasionally things are not as they appear in the boardroom. For example, join me at this ministry's quarterly board meeting.

As board members filed in, everyone smiled and exchanged pleasant greetings. However, when the meeting was called to order, there was no opportunity for board members to transition from their busy lives into their sacred calling as board members. The board chair plunged right into the meeting agenda. There was a brief prayer, then the roll was called and minutes from the previous meeting were reviewed. Up to this point, everything was very cordial.

The next agenda item was one of those heavy-lifting issues (see Lesson 36). After the board chair introduced the matter, one board member staked out a passionate position against the proposal. Then, another member took a very strong position in favor of the proposal. The stage was set for discord.

Some of the ensuing discussion was not very God-honoring, to say the least. Some speeches became too personal. When a vote was taken, the proposal was adopted, with eight in favor and seven against. Even the eight board members voting on the prevailing side left the boardroom with an empty feeling. The seven members who did not prevail were less than satisfied with the result and the tenor of the meeting.

What appeared to be a peaceful start to the board meeting dissolved into an unhealthy exchange between board members with hurt feelings and lasting consequences. The board meeting started routinely, but things were not as they appeared on the surface.

We have been in board meetings when the discussion has become too loud, too shrill, too personal, and more. And, we have seen board chairs respond two ways: 1) simply let the meeting deteriorate, or 2) step up and provide leadership.

Sometimes the board chair must hit the pause button on the meeting and pray. It may require deferring action on a thorny proposal to the next board meeting—even when *Roberts Rules of Order* doesn't provide a clean path to do so.

The sports memorabilia dealer hoped he had a $30,000 baseball but it was really worthless, and he had to cut his losses. There are times in the boardroom when we must cut our losses. In those times, it's not about saving face; it is about conducting God-honoring board work that is fitting and orderly (1 Cor. 14:40).

Investing time in the following three ways are prerequisites for effective board meetings:

- **Invest time for board members to get reacquainted before the meeting starts.** It takes a little time to transition from our personal lives into a board meeting. Start the meeting with a breakfast, lunch, or dinner. Give board members time to share what is happening in their lives.

  If there isn't time to pray, there isn't time for a board meeting.

- **Invest adequate time for prayer before the meeting starts.** The pre-meeting sharing may identify prayer needs. Instead of a perfunctory 60-second prayer by one person, allow all board members the opportunity to lead in prayer, or pray in groups of two or three. If there isn't time to pray, there isn't time for a board meeting.

- **Invest time when tough issues may require multi-meeting exposure.** The larger and more complex the issue, the greater likelihood that discussion of the topic should occur across more than one board meeting. This approach gives the board time to discern together whether or not a proposal is in step with what God wants for the ministry now.

BOARDROOM LESSON

When things are not as they appear to be in the boardroom, it is time for the board chair to restore calm.
Invest time in prayer and enriching relationships so God is honored. This will require strong and sensitive leadership by the board chair.

Board Action Steps:

○ **1. Report:** Ask a board member to read and report on Chapter 18, "The Secret to a Good Meeting Is the Meeting Before the Meeting," in *Leadership Gold: Lessons I've Learned from a Lifetime of Leading* by John C. Maxwell.[2]

○ **2. Read:** Encourage your board chair, with assistance from your CEO, to frequently take the pulse of the meeting and the relationships around the board table.

○ **3. Restore:** When your board meeting abruptly turns from peaceful to rocky, be sure your board chair invests time in restoring calm with all appropriate measures.

Prayer: "Lord, thank you for our board chair. Help our chair foster healthy and God-honoring relationships among our board members so that we encourage our CEO and propel our mission forward. Amen."

16 | DATE BOARD PROSPECTS BEFORE YOU PROPOSE MARRIAGE

He served the shortest board term in the history of the world!

> *God's individual call is normally in line*
> *with the gifts that you already have.*
> *If the ministry's mission is not closely tied to your interests,*
> *your board service will be a draining experience . . .*[1]
>
> John Pellowe

A friend of mine holds the record for "The Shortest Board Term in the History of the World!" I'll call him Tom here (it's a bit embarrassing, so I've changed the details, including his name). His board story is a cautionary warning for other well-intentioned board nominees.

Tom's pastor served on the board of directors of his denomination's Christian camp and he nominated Tom for board service. Tom was honored, and his family loved the camp, so his wife encouraged him to say yes.

The camp's executive director did the usual "blah, blah, blah" recruitment recital at a very nice steak place. He even paid! Tom heard a glowing picture of organizational health, new programs—you know, the usual hype: board service will be a nice addition to his resumé, it will enhance his career, etc. All of this was somehow packaged with appropriate piety.

Tom's detailed description of the meeting was memorable, but then he paused in his story and whispered to me, "So how do I say this delicately? The lunch hour briefing was dismal. In fact, I may have been the first board nominee ever to ask for some pre-meeting orientation, but hey—I believed in the ministry, and I was supporting it financially. So I told him, 'OK. I'm all in.'"

The executive director mentioned that the actual election of board members was just a formality, so in the restaurant parking lot, he opened his trunk, gave Tom four thick binders plus an official camp coffee mug, and slapped him on the back with a big, "Welcome to the board!"

Tom grimaced to me. "Back in my car, I had this gut feeling that I'd made a really, really bad decision, but I soldiered on."

> *At Tom's first board meeting, he counted at least seven cringe moments.*

Have you ever heard of the "cringe factor?" You know, when something abnormal or kind of embarrassing happens in a meeting?

Well, at Tom's first board meeting, he counted at least seven cringe moments. First, the finance committee chair argued over numbers with the CFO. Then the PowerPoint didn't work. Two board members were seriously late and unprepared.

And the worst? Tom said there was more passion, it seemed, for the dinner menu than for the organization's vision and mission. He said it was one "cringe moment" after another.

Tom's succinct bottom line: "I was a fish out of water."

Tom had carpooled with his pastor to his first board meeting, and on the way home that night, his pastor perceptively noticed his silence. He said something like, "That didn't go well, did it?"

"Long story short," Tom admitted to me, "I told my pastor I just couldn't serve. I called the board chair the next morning and resigned. So I guess I hold the record for the shortest board term in the history of the world!"

Tom's story is featured in the video of the *ECFA Governance Toolbox Series No. 1: Recruiting Board Members.*[2] The toolbox describes four best practices to employ when inviting people to consider board service: cultivation, recruitment, orientation, and engagement.

That was Tom's story, and it must have been very embarrassing for the executive director and the board. But more importantly, what was your story when you were invited onto the board? How much time is your governance committee (or nominating committee) investing in the "dating process" for board candidates?

If you're married, it's unlikely that you proposed marriage on your first date. Effective boards don't invite candidates onto the board after just one steak lunch. While Tom could have been an outstanding board member, there was no spiritual discernment process in place. Was it the right time for the camp and for Tom? Was Tom God's choice? There was no discussion of Tom's gifting, strengths, or passion.

John Pellowe notes that "God's individual call is normally in line with the gifts that you already have." He adds, "If the ministry's mission is not closely tied to your interests, your board service will be a draining experience."

Are you called to board service? Pellowe writes, "The Holy Spirit can nudge us towards those good works that God has prepared for us to do (Eph. 2:10); this nudging is usually described as a *call*."[3]

BOARDROOM LESSON
The "hire slower and fire faster" axiom applies to board prospects also. Slow down and take time to spiritually discern if a board candidate's strengths, spiritual gifts, and passion are in alignment with your board's culture and vision.

Board Action Steps:

○ **1. Educate:** Before you invite prospects onto the board, view the 13-minute video and resource materials in the *ECFA Governance Toolbox Series No. 1: Recruiting Board Members.*[4]

○ **2. Establish:** Add to your Board Policies Manual, a paragraph titled "Pathway to the Board," with guidelines for the nominating committee to follow when discerning board prospects.

○ **3. Enrich:** Invest 20 to 30 minutes at your next board meeting to discuss (in small groups), "Ways to Enrich the Four Steps of Board Recruitment: Cultivation, Recruitment, Orientation, and Engagement." (Use the viewing guide in the toolbox series on board recruitment.)

Prayer: "Lord, guide us to the men and women who you have already nudged about serving on our board. Protect us from selecting people who are not your choice at this time. Amen."

17 | SIDETRACK HAREBRAINED IDEAS

Some motions should never gain unmerited oxygen.

> *Dysfunctional directors have their own modus operandi.*
> *Some see themselves as the smartest person in the room,*
> *others seek recognition, and still others are frustrated would-be CEOs.*
> *Whatever their personal motives, they tend to micromanage*
> *or take boardroom discussions down dark alleys.*[1]
>
> Ram Charan, Dennis Carey, and Michael Useem

Have you ever been in the middle of a board meeting when—left-turn, no blinkers—a board member blurts out a harebrained motion to take some drastic action, one that would require much more thought and planning before even being considered?

Perhaps the motion is to increase the board size by 20 members, which, amazingly, is permitted by the bylaws. Or maybe the motion is to have the ministry's three vice presidents report directly to the board, completely bypassing the CEO.

The CEO and the board sit there stunned, hoping against hope that no one will second the motion and it will die the death it deserves. After a few moments of awkward silence, a board member seconds the motion. It was simply a courteous gesture, but didn't his mother tell him that there are exceptions to being courteous? This should have been one of those exceptions.

Before the errant motion was made, the board chair thought the meeting was moving along in fine shape. Then this motion sailed in from left field, acquired a second, and was technically before the board for discussion.

Imagine that you're the board chair. You have two likely scenarios:

> *It was simply a courteous gesture, but didn't his mother tell him that there are exceptions to being courteous?*

- **SCENARIO A:**
  Entertain discussion for the harebrained idea and pray that the motion fails. *Robert's Rules of Order* diehards and most board chairs would definitely go for this option. However, there are some downsides to allowing the motion to be discussed:

  - ☐ **Discussing the crazy motion reinforces over-sensitivity to the maker of the motion.** Perhaps the board member that floated the motion is a new board member and is still finding his or her way through your board protocol (or bureaucracy!). So other board members may be reluctant to deep-six the motion out of sensitivity to this new relationship, and by entertaining the motion, this reluctance is intensified.

    Or perhaps the motion-maker is a major giver to the ministry, and there is some unscripted tip-toeing around this person every time he or she speaks in the boardroom. In either case, the motion gets more legs than it deserves, and the tendency to placate the maker of the motion increases.

☐ **Potential for unintended consequences.**
Harebrained motions rarely pass. However, they may
get unmerited oxygen resulting in a compromise
with the strong support of an "out to lunch" board
member. Perhaps the compromise takes the form of
a new board task force to study the issue. (Hopefully
a standing committee is not formed.) Even a task
force can take on a life of its own and require many
precious hours of board members' time.

- **SCENARIO B:** Sidestepping any discussion of a crazy
motion, with its second, is tricky, but here are two options
for this scenario:

  ☐ **Motion to refer:** The board chair asks for a motion
  to refer the matter to the executive committee, with
  the understanding of most board members that the
  motion will die in the committee.

  ☐ **Motion to table:** The board chair asks for a motion
  to table the matter, with or without intent to kill the
  motion.

  If there is no motion to refer or to table, the board
  chair might table the matter even without a motion
  to table. Now that requires boldness!

It usually takes a bold and experienced chair to take charge
when motions that should never have been introduced
suddenly appear on the boardroom table. How to handle
these motions depends in part on where the motion is
on a scale of one to 10—insensible to sensible.

Bottom line: The sooner any off-the-wall motion is appropriately sidetracked, the sooner board members will be saved from needless agony and wasted time. They will be grateful!

BOARDROOM LESSON

Hopefully, it is the rare moment in your board meetings when motions fly in—not just from left field, but from outer space. Those unusual times will require all the wisdom and courage the board chair can muster to gracefully divert potentially harmful actions.

Board Action Steps:

○ **1. Understand:** The board chair should have an awareness of what constitutes a truly harebrained idea—without this awareness, the chair can be caught by surprise.

○ **2. Prepare:** With the overall awareness of what a motion from outer space looks like, the board chair should be mentally prepared when this occurs.

○ **3. Address:** Even with this preparation, the board chair will need to muster the necessary fortitude to address the issue when it arises.

Prayer: "Lord, give us the courage and wisdom to recognize potential board actions that should never get traction and then to handle them gracefully. Amen."

18 | DO NOT INTERRUPT!

Don't assume board members know how to listen.

Almost all directors look promising
before they enter the boardroom,
but not all perform equally well once inside.[1]

Ram Charan, Dennis Carey, and Michael Useem

We're going to be blunt here, and you can thank us later!

Of the four social styles gathered around your boardroom table (Drivers, Analyticals, Amiables, and Expressives), at least two of the styles prefer to talk more than listen. (And you know who you are—maybe!)

Board members who talk too much are often unaware of their inability to slow down and listen. According to the social style experts,[2] there's a great divide between the preferred pace of most people: how they use their time.

One group favors slowing down:

- **Analyticals** tend to be slow, deliberate, and disciplined.

- **Amiables** tend to be slow but calm and often undisciplined.

The other group keeps the agenda moving:

- **Drivers** tilt toward being swift and efficient but impatient.

- **Expressives** tend to be rapid and quick but undisciplined.

All four styles (that's how God created us) will likely show up in your boardroom. It takes great skill and insight—a deep understanding of the pluses and minuses of the four social styles—to consistently create a boardroom culture that is respectful and God-honoring.

Good news—there's help! Ruth Haley Barton offers 10 listening guidelines in her important book *Pursuing God's Will Together: A Discernment Practice for Leadership Groups.*[3] Leverage those guidelines, and in just a few minutes, you can facilitate an insightful exercise at the beginning of your next board meeting.

Barton writes, "Don't take it for granted that people know how to listen. We

"Do not formulate what you want to say while someone else is speaking."

live in a culture where people are much more skilled at trying to get their point across and arguing their position than they are at engaging in mutually influencing relationships."

Barton concludes this powerful page on listening guidelines with a personal reflection challenge:

> Invite God to search you and reveal your normal patterns of speaking and listening. Ask him to reveal one aspect of this kind of listening that you could practice in order to be a more helpful listener in leadership discernment.

10 Guidelines for Entering Into and Maintaining a Listening Posture

☑ Check the ONE guideline that is most challenging for you:

❑ 1. Take full advantage of the opportunity provided to become settled in God's presence.

❑ 2. Listen to others with your entire self (senses, feelings, intuition, imagination, and rational faculties).

❑ 3. Do not interrupt.

❑ 4. Pause between speakers to absorb what has been said.

❑ 5. Do not formulate what you want to say while someone else is speaking.

❑ 6. Speak for yourself, expressing your own thoughts and feelings, referring to your own experiences. Avoid being hypothetical. Steer away from making broad generalizations.

❑ 7. Do not challenge what others say. Rather, ask good questions that enable you to wonder about things together.

❑ 8. Listen to the group as a whole—to those who have spoken aloud as well as to those who haven't. If you notice that someone hasn't spoken, feel free to ask what he or she is thinking. Some people aren't as comfortable as others at asserting themselves in conversation, but when space is created for them to speak, they have much to offer because they have been listening and observing quietly.

❑ 9. Leave space for anyone who may want to speak a first time before speaking a second time yourself.

❑ 10. Hold your desires and opinions—even your convictions—lightly. Be willing to be influenced by others whom you respect.

Taken from *Pursuing God's Will Together* by Ruth Haley Barton. Copyright (c) 2012 by Ruth Haley Barton. Used by permission of InterVarsity Press, P.O. Box 1400, Downers Grove, IL 60515-1426. www.ivpress.com

BOARDROOM LESSON

Invest time in helping board members improve
their listening skills and thereby improve the culture
in your boardroom.

Board Action Steps:

○ 1. **Read:** Around the boardroom, ask each board member
to read one listening guideline (in order, from one to
ten). Then in groups of two, ask each person to identify
the guideline that is most challenging for them.

○ 2. **Review:** Invite one board member in advance of the
board meeting to study and review Chapter 11 in
Pursuing God's Will Together by Ruth Haley Barton.[4]
Then pray in groups of two.

○ 3. **Lead:** Inspire your board chair to lead graciously.
Create a boardroom culture that expects the board
chair to address inappropriate boardroom conduct,
including people who talk too much.

Prayer: "Lord, forgive me for talking when I should be
listening—especially to You. Amen."

PART 6:

BOARDROOM TIME-WASTERS, TROUBLEMAKERS, AND TRUTH-TELLERS

In our experience,
as many as half of *Fortune* 500 companies
have one or two dysfunctional directors.[1]

Ram Charan, Dennis Carey, and Michael Useem

19 | NEVER THROW RED MEAT ON THE BOARD TABLE

Boards need advance preparation to fully address complex issues.

> *When time isn't taken for precise motion clarity,*
> *there can be several different perceptions*
> *of what is really being discussed*
> *and nobody knows exactly what will show up*
> *in the official minutes.*[1]
>
> Cathy Leimbach

We've observed our fair share of boardroom time-wasters and troublemakers. A common, and very unnecessary, time-waster is something akin to throwing raw meat on the board table.

In this time-wasting scenario, the CEO brings a tough issue to the board without a written recommendation for board action—in fact, there is no recommendation at all, written or unwritten.

So the board starts with a blank page on this particular issue. After a lengthy discussion of all the options, a motion is finally floated. There is more discussion. Then the motion is withdrawn, and another motion is offered. Amendments follow, and with some discomfort, the board finally approves a resolution. Or, after all this work, the board refers the matter to the executive committee for more study.

The final action more closely resembled a gerrymandered political map than a finely tuned resolution. So sad—and unnecessary.

By starting from scratch, the process consumes 90 minutes of the board meeting—perhaps double the time that might have been spent if the board had started with a well-thought-out recommendation and a draft of a resolution.

Red meat on the boardroom table is usually a no-no. Boards want, need, and prefer that the "cooking" has already begun. If a board must create its own starting point, it can be a very painful process that ultimately diminishes productivity.

Without adequate advance preparation to fully address an issue, boards tend to function as a committee of the whole, often resorting to painfully circuitous discussion. It can result in floating a resolution only to have it amended multiple times while the boardroom clock continues to tick, tick, tick.

There is a better way. It may be a regular meeting or a specially called meeting. It may be an in-person or virtual meeting. Either way, the key players are the board chair and the CEO as together they prepare for the topic to be addressed by the board.

Many board issues are routine and do not require special preparation. For example, the audit report goes to the audit committee or finance committee for their review. That committee will typically send the audit report to the full board, at which time they will generally receive the report.

Other issues are so complex that they require wisdom and discernment to decide how to properly prepare them for the board. In most of these situations, the staff is well qualified to draft the resolutions with review by the board chair.

Without adequate advance preparation to fully address an issue, boards tend to function as a committee of the whole, often resorting to painfully circuitous discussion.

Here is the key principle: Always submit recommended resolutions to the board for every action item. The draft of each resolution should be carefully prepared.

Wordsmithing resolutions in a calm, pressure-free environment before a board meeting can be challenging enough. But writing a resolution on a complex topic from scratch in a board meeting with the clock ticking—well, that can be a significant challenge. Even if the draft resolution is amended, the final version will probably include much of the carefully crafted language from the draft.

Accompanying every draft resolution should be an appropriate preamble to provide the context for each resolution. While the board may amend the resolution or fail to adopt it, a well-prepared preamble and resolution will provide clarity to the issue and will often save the board significant time. The inclusion of a preamble with a motion will serve the board well. When a motion is reviewed years later, the preamble helps explain why the board adopted the revolution.

Here is an example of a draft resolution with preamble that ties into the ministry's Board Policies Manual (see Lesson 4):

> Whereas it is desirable to enhance the responsibilities of the audit committee to require at least an annual meeting with the ministry's independent auditors,
>
> Resolved that the following text shall be added to section 3.7.3 of the Board Policies Manual: "The audit committee shall also meet with the organization's independent auditors at least once a year; for at least a portion of the meeting, all members of the staff shall be excused from the proceedings."

Tired of time-wasters? The advance preparation approach is essential for in-person board meetings.

Thinking of saving time with a virtual board meeting? Then note this: The importance of advance preparation increases exponentially for virtual board meetings. Introducing an important agenda topic with a blank page is unthinkable for a complex issue, especially in a virtual setting where communication between board members is even more challenging.

BOARDROOM LESSON

Adequate advance preparation of resolutions
for board consideration will contribute positively
to effective, efficient board deliberations and actions.

Board Action Steps:

○ 1. **Reflect:** Review the advance board materials for the last few board meetings.

○ 2. **Improve:** Determine if the advance preparations for board actions can be improved.

○ 3. **Act:** Commit to prepare advance drafts of resolutions to correspond with every recommended action.

Prayer: "Lord, may our board meeting preparations enhance the work we do for you. Amen."

20 | APPLY FOR A STAFF POSITION AND YOU CAN DEAL WITH THAT ISSUE!

Help board members not to cross the line into operational details.

Execution is where management starts and the board stops.[1]

Ram Charan, Dennis Carey, and Michael Useem

In nearly every board meeting, one board member will want to drill into the minutiae.

In one meeting, Tim, an attorney, asked about details of the ministry's hotel contract for a fundraising event. He was concerned that the ministry had committed to meals that were overly expensive.

In another meeting, Rachel, a development professional, requested a detailed analysis of gifts received from each of the last five fundraising letters.

In yet another meeting, April, an IT consultant, wanted a step-by-step report on measures the ministry had taken to avoid security breaches.

Finally (and to no surprise!), David, the ministry's CEO, reached his limit. When one more board member drilled deeply into operational details with probing questions,

David said kindly yet very directly, "Apply for a staff position, and you can deal with that issue." David had learned that some questions are meant to be answered; other questions are simply meant to be admired.

David's board chair could have and should have been his protector, shielding him from the intrusions by board members into areas of David's responsibilities. Technically, a board member has the right to ask any question in the book. Practically speaking, however, a steady habit of board members veering across the line into operational matters will likely drive any CEO right over the edge.

Board members wallow in operational details far too often. With sophisticated boards, dipping a toe into operations may only happen occasionally. With less accomplished boards, it happens all the time.

At least three things happen when board meeting discussions regularly detour into operations:

- **Time is squandered.** When a board member meddles in operational details, the board's collective time is wasted. Consider the hourly rate of each of the board members. Then multiply the combined hourly rate by the time wasted in board meetings when the discussion veers away from policy and other critical issues. The resulting number can be astounding.

- **Decision-making boundaries are crossed.** When the board veers into operational discussions, a bright line has been crossed by addressing topics that should be reserved for the CEO.

- **Frustration will be the result.** When the board travels down the operational highway, some members of the board may be frustrated, but the CEO will be *very* frustrated. This creates such operational dizziness that most CEOs will then ask for a time-out to address this out-of-control journey.

So how can a board avoid the operational meddling disease? Discernment is key, and there are at least two solutions:

> *What happens when board meeting discussions regularly detour into operations? It squanders time that should be devoted to major issues, blurs decision-making, and impacts the emotional well-being of CEOs and board members.*

- **Solution No. 1: Inspire each board member to be discerning and sensitive to the issue.** It is up to each board member to be spiritually discerning and highly sensitive about which topics they comment on during board meetings. If each board member exercises care to avoid operational matters, this will go a long way to resolve this concern.

- **Solution No. 2: Empower the board chair to address operational overreach.** This can be positioned two ways:

  - □ **Setting the agenda.** The agenda sets the tone for the level of the board meeting discussions. If the agenda properly avoids operational areas, this is the first and best line of defense to prevent such discussions from occurring.

☐ **Monitoring board discussions.** It is during the actual board meetings, of course, when board members face the greatest temptation to delve into operational matters. The board chair must monitor this primary challenge and urge members to "flee temptation."

Any board member can and should throw a flag when the discussion lapses into operations. It's as simple as this: "Madame Chairperson, it seems to me that we have just crossed the line into an operational topic, and we should respect the right of our CEO to handle such issues."

Even though every board member can raise a concern about the level of the board discussion, the primary responsibility rests squarely on the board chair. He or she is the first line of defense for keeping discussions at the appropriate level. If the board chair carries out this responsibility, it will save the CEO from the awkward situation of having to throw a flag.

There are few issues that will cause more friction between the board and the CEO than the board delving into operational issues. When boards ignore this important issue, they do so at their own peril.

BOARDROOM LESSON

Sound governance requires that all board members
understand and apply the principle of exiting
the operational highway and trusting such matters
to the CEO.

Board Action Steps:

○ 1. **Inquire:** Review the discussions and actions of the last
few board meetings to determine if the board ever
crossed the line into operational matters.

○ 2. **Identify:** If the board migrated into operational areas,
identify the reasons why this happened. This may
include identifying the guilty board members.

○ 3. **Inspire:** Commit to keeping board discussions and
decisions at a high level.

Prayer: "Lord, help us bless our CEO by staying on the
governance highway and not veering onto the operational
highway. Amen."

21 | BACK OFF THE LEDGE OF DYSFUNCTIONAL MAYHEM

When dysfunction reigns, healthy board members head for the door.

> *If you board the wrong train*
> *it is no use running along the corridor*
> *in the opposite direction.*[1]
>
> Dietrich Bonhoeffer

Your board is blessed when the board chair and CEO can blend truth-telling with God-honoring grace. Here are six board members who need a wake-up call:

- **Abby** only shows up at every other board meeting. She always has a plausible excuse, but her attendance ratio is only 50 percent.

- **Carl** never reviews the materials provided before the meeting. As a result, the board must endure his endless questions during the meeting—questions he could have answered for himself if only he had studied the preliminary materials.

- **Betty** and **Quincy** cannot seem to get along with each other. In nearly every meeting, they lock horns in a demonstration that does not evidence the fruits of the Spirit.

- **Heather** brings a superiority complex to most meetings. She takes the position of an expert on every agenda item. When she begins to wax eloquent, other board members just roll their eyes.

- **Bill** regularly insists on wading into operational matters that are the purview of the CEO. The board chair continually attempts to bring Bill back to board-level discussions, but Bill just can't seem to help himself.

What do Abby, Carl, Betty, Quincy, Heather, and Bill have in common? They distract the board from its responsibilities. Other board members wonder, with so many dysfunctional members, is it really worth their time to serve on this board?

What does a board do when it is on the verge of dysfunctional mayhem? Should a board address discipline issues or let them fester? Most boards go with "fester" and trudge along with no relief in sight.

What does a board do when it is on the verge of dysfunctional mayhem? Should a board address discipline issues or let them fester? Most boards go with "fester" and trudge along with no relief in sight.

Without a course correction, the only ray of hope is to wait until term limits cycle out and then replace problem board members. That is, if the board has term limits in effect. If not, and Abby and friends are lifers, the festering takes on a life of its own.

Of course, the better choice is to address dysfunction, even though that may be the most painful route in the short-term. Here are four strategic steps:

- **Step 1. Assess the dysfunction.** Who is causing the most significant disruption on the board? What are the most important issues that need to be addressed and when?

- **Step 2. Evaluate the level of dysfunction.** This is a topic for the board chair, the CEO, and the governance committee to evaluate. Together, do they have the willingness to step up and do the hard, perhaps painful, work in seeking to change the board's destructive direction?

- **Step 3. Develop a game plan.** Decide which issues should be addressed first. Develop a priority plan and decide who will address them. For some board members, it may be best for the board chair to meet with the member alone. For others, the board chair and the CEO may wish to meet together with the board member.

- **Step 4. Roll up your sleeves and expect resolution.** Pray for these outcomes:

  - ☐ **"Absentee Abby."** The board chair met with Abby, and she readily admitted that her attendance was subpar. Because of her schedule, she could not commit to improve her attendance record. The board chair suggested Abby step off the board and consider rejoining it if time permitted in the future. She agreed and submitted her resignation. *Bless her!*

  - ☐ **"Clueless Carl."** The meeting with Carl was more challenging. He really believed he was adequately reviewing board materials before the meeting. While he said he would try to do better, the commitment seemed shallow. *Progress!*

☐ **"Bickering Betty"** and **"Quarrelsome Quincy."**
This meeting was the most sensitive of all. They both felt their boardroom banter was just an extension of their personalities. They were surprised that other board members felt they were crossing a line with their verbal exchanges. However, they did agree to be more careful in their boardroom communication. *Grace abounds!*

☐ **"High-Horse Heather."** The meeting with Heather was not a walk in the park either. She resented the board chair questioning her attitude toward other board members. As the meeting progressed, she became increasingly agitated and at the mid-way point, she resigned. *A good conclusion!*

☐ **"Bottleneck Bill."** During this meeting, Bill clearly did not agree with the board chair and the CEO that his discussions were taking the board into the weeds. However, during the meeting, it seemed that the Holy Spirit was opening his eyes. He promised to work on his approach to board topics. *Thank You, Lord, for opening his eyes!*

So, this resulted in two resignations, three significant commitments to improve, and one response that was somewhat tepid. This hard work gives the board the opportunity to select two new qualified board members, and four other members were given a gentle nudge to step up in their commitment to good governance. The board chair and the CEO get two thumbs up for their work.

Monitoring aberrations in the board room is not easy. However, the options are clear: gently encourage board members to stay within reasonable boardroom guardrails or let boardroom issues fester and reap the results.

BOARDROOM LESSON

Will you address serious board issues or let them fester? Let's face it—there are no perfect boards, and there are no perfect board members. Governance is an imperfect process. However, addressing board dysfunctions in the short term promises a much better opportunity to be a high-performing board in the long term.

Board Action Steps:

○ 1. **Prepare:** Ask board members to sign an annual affirmation statement that communicates God-honoring core values, giving board leadership an obvious basis to open a conversation about a member's dysfunction. (See Lesson 31.)

○ 2. **Discern:** When you observe significant dysfunctions in the boardroom, commit to a prayer and discernment period before you stir the pot.

Prayer: "Lord, grant us the wisdom and the strength to address boardroom issues gracefully but head-on. Amen."

PART 7:

BOARDROOM
BEST PRACTICES

The ancient Romans had a tradition.
Whenever one of their engineers constructed an arch,
as the capstone was hoisted into place,
the engineer assumed accountability for his work
in the most profound way possible; he stood under the arch.[1]

Michael Armstrong

22 | THE MOST UNDERRATED BOARD POSITION

The position of the board chair is pivotal to a healthy board.

> *Underlying the professional qualifications for the board chair are three sensitive areas of board leadership that depend directly on personal character . . . integrity, trust, and humility.*[1]
>
> David McKenna

How is the board chair chosen for your ministry? For a few ministries, the founder is the leader and the board chair. But for most ministries, the board chair is elected by the board.

But what happens before the election? Is there an appropriate amount of planning leading up to the election? Or is it a last-minute decision involving little discernment?

In a worst-case scenario, the person chosen to be the board chair is the only person who is willing to serve. Or, the fourth vice chair moves up to become the third vice chair. The third vice chair becomes the second vice chair, and the second vice chair becomes the chair whether qualified or not. You get the idea.

The board's approach to selecting its chair speaks volumes about the importance the board places on this key position.

Moreover, the quality of the chair selection process may well determine the effectiveness of the board. Whatever the process, *without* the call of God on the board chair, we cannot expect the chair to give the task the highest priority of time, energy, and resources.

Is the board chair just another board position—an equal among equals? *Hardly!*

According to David McKenna, the board chair must be *first* among equals. Underlying the professional qualifications for the board chair are three sensitive areas of board leadership that depend directly on personal character:

- The board chair must be first among equals in *integrity*. While every board member must possess high moral and ethical standards, the character of the board chair is the most visible. The ministry's top leader is the public face of the organization, but the chair is the face of the board.

- The board chair must be first among equals in *trust*. The board chair must also have the gift of diplomacy. Yet more important than diplomacy is the gift of building relationships based on trust—relationships with the ministry's top leader, the entire board, the standing committees, the task forces, and each individual member.

- The board chair must be first among equals in *humility*. The title of board chair sounds lofty, yet it comes with no inherent authority or power. It is only the board itself that authorizes the chair to speak or act on its behalf.

The board chair may be the holder of a prestigious title, wielder of a ready gavel, collaborator with the CEO, announcer of good and bad news, voice of the board, or the power behind the scene. No matter how the board chair role is described, it is the key position of the board.

The competencies expected for a board chair are indicative of the importance of the position:

- Personal integrity and public credibility

- Passionate commitment and understanding of the organization's mission

  If you want a healthy board, choose a board chair who is first among equals.

- Executive leadership accomplishments

- Service in a leadership position of the board (e.g., committee chair or executive committee member)

- Earned respect of board members, the CEO, and key stakeholders

- Diplomatic skills in building relationships, handling conflict, and building consensus

- Communication skills, oral and written, with the ability to listen, elicit diverse responses, reconcile differences

- Willingness and ability to commit time to the leadership of the organization

The board chair has many faces and functions. Here are just a few: missionary, model, mentor, manager, moderator, mediator, monitor, and master. But chief among all roles is that of maestro, explains McKenna in *Call of the Chair*.[2]

Leading from the board chair is like being the conductor of an orchestra. A conductor must imagine the sound of the music when all the instruments are playing as one. Like an orchestra, each board member must be reading from the same page.

The conductor must "listen to the clarinet," perhaps the most forgotten instrument in a symphony. Likewise, the board chair must be sure more quiet board members are heard and that all board members are listening to each other.

Can an orchestra play great music without a conductor relying on gifted instrumentalists who own the score? Perhaps. "But if it is to soar into the realm of the artistic vision, it needs the conductor."[3]

"A board of gifted volunteers who are committed to the mission can excel as a working body. However, if the board is to rise to its spiritual potential, it needs a chair who brings the personal experience of Pentecost to the leadership of the board."[4]

BOARDROOM LESSON

Too often, the selection of the board chair does not receive the priority it deserves. The attitude that just any board member is qualified to chair the board removes the possibility that the board will reach its maximum potential.

Board Action Steps:

○ 1. **Read:** Ask your board chair and CEO to read and discuss *Call of the Chair* by David McKenna.

○ 2. **Review:** Take time to review your process of selecting the board chair.

○ 3. **Reflect:** How could the board chair selection process be improved?

Prayer: "Lord, help us discern who should be the next leader for our board, the person who will be the face of the board and whose life exemplifies integrity, trust, and humility. Amen."

23 | FOCUS ON MISSION IMPACT *AND* SUSTAINABILITY

The "dual bottom line" equips boards to address dead horses and sacred cows (or goats).

Dakota tribal wisdom says that when you discover you are riding a dead horse, the best strategy is to dismount.[1]

Elmer Towns and Warren Bird

Imagine you're on this board. The country leader of an international sports ministry is handing the baton to a younger leader—a good thing. But he pleads, "Please don't terminate the goat ministry!" (Ever notice when a program is struggling, it's usually called a "ministry"?)

I was the third party asked to address the elephant in the room about the goat ministry. (Sorry, I couldn't resist mixing metaphors.)

Me: "Does the goat program have high impact or provide revenue for your sports ministry?"

Leader: "No, but I'm hoping it will someday."

I was reminded of my two favorite one-liners on nonprofit sustainability:

- "We're nonprofit, but we didn't plan it that way."

- "Nonprofit is a tax designation, not a management philosophy."

We've listened to hundreds of nonprofit staff members whine, "Yeah, but are we a ministry or a business?" (Their answer is in their question and the way they intone that nasty B-word.)

That's the wrong question. Scripture doesn't confuse us with a negative dichotomy between business and ministry. The better question is, "Whatever tax code we use to serve others (nonprofit or for-profit), will we be sustainable and God-honoring in the long-term?"

The goat scenario only needed a one-word response: "Stop."

Lesson 23, for many board members, might be a favorite best-practice takeaway. Three nonprofit experts have adapted the classic, four-quadrant business growth grid to help nonprofit leaders and boards focus on sustainability issues. It's simple to understand but highly demanding of the board's best wisdom and spiritual discernment.

In *Nonprofit Sustainability*, the big idea from coauthors Jeanne Bell, Jan Masaoka, and Steve Zimmerman pops out on page 25 with their brilliant chart, "Dual Bottom Line: Mission Impact and Financial Sustainability."[2]

And by the way, have you ever noticed that page 25 is often a great summary of a well-written book? After 24 pages of introduction and warm up, the authors often deliver the meat and potatoes on page 25.

For example, in John Frank's short book, *Stewardship as a Lifestyle*, page 25 includes an excellent chart on 12 factors in

"God's Eternal Economic Equation."[3] In writing this chapter, Pearson checked out page 25 in Busby's book *TRUST: The Firm Foundation for Kingdom Fruitfulness*,[4] and bingo! Page 25 delivers a hilarious story, a memorable Winston Churchill quotation, and three preachable points on why truth-telling is vital to creating trust in Christ-centered ministries. (Full disclosure: author John reviewed page 25 in his own book, *Mastering the Management Buckets* and didn't find much!)

The dual bottom line chart in *Nonprofit Sustainability* is part Nonprofit 101 and part Harvard Business School. The authors write that getting to nonprofit sustainability involves three steps: 1) The Matrix Map Analysis, 2) Decision Making, and 3) The Sustainable Nonprofit Business Model.

Dual Bottom Line:
Mission Impact and Financial Sustainability

High Mission Impact
Low Sustainability

High Mission Impact
High Sustainability

Low Mission Impact
Low Sustainability

Low Mission Impact
High Sustainability

Chart adapted from *Nonprofit Sustainability: Making Strategic Decisions for Financial Viability*[5] (Used by permission.)

At your next board meeting or annual review of your strategic plan, ask your CEO to plot the ministry's key programs into these four quadrants. "The Dual Bottom Line" matrix map will help you visualize mission impact and financial sustainability:

Are you tempted to prolong a program that will never be sustainable—perhaps unduly swayed by your heart?

- **Stars** (High Mission Impact, High Sustainability): Are you investing adequate budget and staff to ensure these programs will continue to be stars?

- **Hearts** (High Mission Impact, Low Sustainability): Are you tempted to prolong a program here that will never be sustainable—perhaps unduly swayed by your heart? These programs may be core to your mission, but you must address the sustainability issues.

- **Money Tree** (Low Mission Impact, High Sustainability): Heed Peter Drucker's wisdom: "Never subordinate the mission in order to get money."[6] But if, like a rescue mission, your thrift store generates a substantial surplus to support the "heart" side of the ministry, then feed it!

- **Stop Sign** (Low Mission Impact, Low Sustainability): This is so easy for some board members: "Stop the bleeding!" Yet, it's excruciatingly painful for others, especially founders: "Give it more time!" So pray, discern, and also address the "Top-10 Questions to Ask About Program Capacity and Sustainability" in *Mastering the Management Buckets*.[7] It's especially important to ask, "Under what conditions do we agree that we will pull 'the plug' on this program if the goals are not achieved by the target date?"

In Luke 14:28-30, Jesus had this to say about sustainability: "Is there anyone here who, planning to build a new house, doesn't first sit down and figure the cost so you'll know if you can complete it? If you only get the foundation laid and then run out of money, you're going to look pretty foolish. Everyone passing by will poke fun at you: 'He started something he couldn't finish'" (MSG).

BOARDROOM LESSON

The "dual bottom line" exercise equips boards to address dead horses and sacred cows (or goats). Plot your ministry's key programs in the four-quadrant impact/sustainability grid, then discern next steps.

Board Action Steps:

○ 1. **Read:** *Nonprofit Sustainability: Making Strategic Decisions for Financial Viability* by Jeanne Bell, Jan Masaoka, and Steve Zimmerman.

○ 2. **Plot:** Ask your CEO to plot your major programs within the four quadrants for the board's review.

○ 3. **Assess:** Discern what should be done with each program, especially asking if you are investing in and growing your stars.

Prayer: "Lord, we've been negligent in starting programs, without counting the cost. We did it in your name but without your direction. Forgive us. Amen."

24 | MINISTRY FUNDRAISING 101 FOR BOARD MEMBERS

Could your board members pass a pop-quiz on fundraising practices?

> *Our board paid little attention to how the ministry raised gifts.*
> *We only tracked giving trends.*
> *Then one day, the CEO informed us that we had been sued*
> *for not fulfilling the restrictions for a major gift.*
> *That was the day our board became much more involved*
> *in the funding practices.*

One of the most important roles of a board is to understand the overall fundraising practices for the ministry. Without proper gift funding, most ministries cannot successfully serve the needs of their program recipients.

The board should ensure that the ministry's fundraising practices are ethical and reflect well on the ministry and its mission.

These six areas are critical for the board to understand:

1. **Temporarily restricted gifts.** Most ministries receive temporarily restricted gifts. Some receive only a few of these gifts, while others receive significant levels of them. Though some temporarily restricted gifts are received

without any solicitation by the ministry, they are still restricted gifts. Other ministries actively solicit and receive temporarily restricted gifts.

Lawsuits are increasingly filed by givers who believe the restrictions they placed on significant gifts were not honored. Ministry boards are responsible for ensuring that these funds are used in a timely manner for the purposes identified by the giver. Any financial reports received by the board should:

☐ Identify any unexpended temporarily restricted gifts and project when the funds will be expended.

☐ Indicate the use of restricted gifts during the reporting period in sufficient detail to enable the board to determine if restricted gift purposes are being met.

Lawsuits are increasingly filed by givers who believe the restrictions they placed on significant gifts were not honored.

If temporarily restricted gifts are received and/or solicited for international programs, the board takes on even more responsibility than if the gifts are expended domestically. Why? It is generally much more challenging to provide adequate oversight of international expenditures.

2. **Gift acceptance policy.** The board should receive a copy of the ministry's gift acceptance policy. If no policy exists, one should be adopted.[1]

From time to time, the ministry may be offered donations that compromise the ministry's ethics, financial circumstances, program focus, or other interests.

A sound gift acceptance policy provides standards and procedures for determining when a ministry will or will not accept a donation. Staff should at least annually confirm to the board that the gift acceptance policy has been carefully followed.

3. **Fundraising techniques.** The ministry's most valuable asset is its good name. If a ministry engages in questionable fundraising practices, it can quickly forfeit a good name that took years to build. The board should know if the ministry is employing fundraising techniques that are coercive, intimidating, or intended to harass potential givers.

4. **Compensation for fundraisers.** Does the ministry follow ECFA[2] and AFP (Association of Fundraising Professionals)[3] standards by avoiding compensating internal or external fundraisers based on a percentage of the gifts raised? This unacceptable practice can allow the fundraiser to place his or her own interests ahead of ministry interests. This could jeopardize givers' trust in the ministry. Performance-based pay that includes pay for reaching certain funding thresholds is allowable as long as it is not based on a percentage of gifts raised.

5. **Charitable solicitation laws.** Most states regulate the solicitation of contributions by charitable organizations.

Therefore, unless they qualify for an exemption, ministries must register with each state in which they solicit funds. The board is responsible to ensure compliance with the various charitable solicitation laws.

6. **Privacy policy.** Except where disclosure is required by law, most ministries have a policy that they will not sell or otherwise make available the names and contact information of givers. The board should understand the ministry's privacy policy and receive an annual confirmation that the policy is being followed.

For a ministry that receives a significant amount of charitable gifts, few board responsibilities are more important than providing oversight of the fundraising process. Far too often, boards inappropriately absolve themselves of this duty, assuming these matters are being adequately overseen by the CEO.

BOARDROOM LESSON

The board should have a thorough understanding of the ministry's fundraising program—both how funds are raised and how restricted funds are used. If gifts are expended internationally, the responsibility ramps up exponentially.

Board Action Steps:

○ 1. **Read:** Ask a board member to read and report on *The Guide to Charitable Giving for Churches and Ministries* by Dan Busby, Michael Martin, and John Van Drunen.[4]

○ 2. **Review:** Be sure that giver-restricted gifts are expended on a timely basis and consistently with giver restrictions.

○ 3. **Comply:** Confirm that the ministry is in compliance with State Charitable Solicitation laws and its gift acceptance and privacy policies.

Prayer: "Lord, help our board faithfully carry out its responsibility to provide oversight of the ministry's fundraising program. Amen."

PART 8:

BOARDROOM
WORST PRACTICES

MINUTES OF OUR APRIL BOARD MEETING

The year's delay in producing an annual report is
because the advertising agency that agreed to do the layout
on a volunteer basis got lucky and has some paid work.

While in executive session, the Board also votes
to move the office and revise the letterhead.[1]

Brian O'Connell

25 ALIGN BOARD MEMBER STRENGTHS WITH COMMITTEE ASSIGNMENTS

Leverage the Three Powerful S's.

> *If you are not strong enough to state your position on an issue, remember that God places people on boards because of who he made them to be, the experiences he gave them, their education, or their perspectives; he wants the contribution that only they can make to be a benefit to this particular ministry at this particular time.* [1]
>
> John Pellowe

"Mr. Chairman, with all due respect…"

Whenever a board member begins with, "Mr. Chairman, with all due respect…," you know something very interesting will follow!

I'll never forget that moment. The room got quiet. The chairman's mouth dropped. Every board member focused on their colleague at the other end of the boardroom.

It was the very first board meeting of a new nonprofit ministry. Throwing best governance practices, due diligence, and caution to the wind, the CEO/founder had personally recruited every board member, but many had never met each other!

(Rule No. 1: Before agreeing to serve on a board, meet the other board members first to discern their passion for the ministry, heart for God, character, and governance experience.)

The CEO/founder, in his first stint as a nonprofit chief executive officer, had retained me as a consultant. Apparently, he was a bit wary that I would say too much in his first board meeting, as his instructions were clear and blunt: "Just sit in that chair [not at the board table] and observe the meeting. You can share your feedback with me after board members have exited."

I dutifully observed from the perimeter, but it was hard to keep quiet. I mean, I had so much to offer!

So in this speed-through-the-agenda environment by the old-school board chair, committee assignments were announced. There was no advance agreement on the continuum between policy-making governance versus hands-on governance. Depending on the board's style, maybe some committees would not be needed.

Board members had not been consulted in advance about committee assignments. It was recruitment by fiat. The only thing missing was a black robe and a banging gavel.

And that's when "Frank" interrupted the board chair. You could hear a pin drop!

"Mr. Chairman, with all due respect…" Frank paused. "I appreciate your confidence in me that I could serve on that committee, but honestly, that area is not one of my strengths."

If this had been on video, camera two would have captured a close-up of the consultant in the back of the room. Big smile. Maybe with a hint of "I told you so." I couldn't resist. I couldn't pass up this delicious, teachable moment.

I sprang to my feet with an arms-wide gesture to my new favorite board member and blurted out, "Wow, everyone! Did you hear what Frank just said? He said that his committee assignment did not align with his strengths! *Oh, my!* Can you imagine the incredible culture you could create for this important ministry if the board modeled a strengths-based environment for staff, volunteers, donors, and your customers?"

> "Imagine if you served on committees that leveraged your strengths. You'd be six times as likely to be engaged in your board work. Wow!"

Trust me. I didn't look at my former friend, the CEO/founder, or the board chair. I just kept preaching while I had the pulpit.

"Imagine if right from the get-go, all board members were inspired (and permitted) to leverage their *Three Powerful S's:*

- Strengths (from Gallup's bestselling *StrengthsFinder 2.0*[2] book and assessment)

- Social Styles (know your style and other board members' styles: Analytical, Driving, Amiable, or Expressive[3])

- **S**piritual Gifts (Romans 12, Ephesians 4, 1 Corinthians 12, etc.)

"Imagine if you served on committees that leveraged your strengths. You'd be *six times as likely* to be engaged in your board work. Wow!

"Gallup says that people (and I would add board members) 'who *do* have the opportunity to focus on their strengths every day are *six times as likely to be engaged in their jobs* and more than *three times as likely to report having an excellent quality of life in general.*'[4]

"So, Frank, thanks for having this insight about yourself, and thanks for modeling this with conviction to other board members!"

I sat down, and after a few harrumphs, the chairman got his train back on schedule and finished the agenda.

Did I mention that was my last day as their consultant?

It was worth it!

BOARDROOM LESSON

Avoid committee appointments by fiat. Instead, leverage the *Three Powerful S's* of each board member (their Strengths, Social Styles, and Spiritual Gifts). According to Gallup, "People who do have the opportunity to focus on their strengths every day are six times as likely to be engaged in their jobs and more than three times as likely to report having an excellent quality of life in general."

Board Action Steps:

○ 1. **Identify:** Give every board member the book, *StrengthsFinder 2.0* by Tom Rath, and inspire them to complete the online assessment which identifies their top five strengths.

○ 2. **Inspire:** When discerning committee assignments, challenge board members to serve on committees that leverage their strengths, their social styles, their spiritual gifts, and their passions.

○ 3. **Invite:** Create a board culture that affirms members for speaking up, even when the discussion might be uncomfortable or unpopular.

Prayer: "Lord, the Psalmist wrote that 'we are fearfully and wonderfully made.' Guide all of us as we seek to leverage our God-given strengths and gifts. Amen."

26 | SPOTTING, CATCHING, OR EXITING A FALLING CEO[1]

Watch for the critical signs.

It was obvious to many others that our CEO was utterly failing, but our board was blind to what was happening right before our very eyes.

Kent was in his seventh year as the ministry's CEO when questions began to arise about his leadership.

Up to that point, the board had been very comfortable with Kent. There was great synergy between the board and the CEO.

However, Kent did not allow any staff members to be in the boardroom, so the board had little contact with the staff. Board members did not visit program sites, so they were generally disconnected from the services provided by the ministry.

A vacuum of board involvement and information was the backdrop for what appeared to be a successful CEO who was actually failing. The board had accepted an environment with reduced opportunity for the board to spot or catch a falling CEO.

Matters turned so bad in Kent's eighth, ninth, and tenth years as the CEO that the board terminated him at the end of that period. It should have happened several years earlier.

The board had reached step 11 in their 12-step self-denial program before they could admit the mistakes they had made in the process. When they were finally able to be introspective, it was clear that they should have spotted the warning signs along the way.

What the board missed: The sudden departure of highly valued staff members should have set off alarm bells.

It all started with the executive search that resulted in Kent being chosen as the CEO. Board members spent significant time on the long and intensive process. When the final five candidates were presented by the search firm, the search committee did not have high enthusiasm for any of the five, but they held their nose and recommended Kent to the board.

The board should have sent the search firm back to the drawing board to bring them more candidates. However, it had taken so much time and money to get to this point that they couldn't imagine starting over. Plus, the search firm had told them that the five finalists were all excellent candidates. Though they may have been good candidates, they were not the right candidates for the position. In the end, Kent was hired.

Kent entered the sacred two-year CEO honeymoon period, when CEOs can nearly do no wrong. During this time, the board was euphoric over their excellent choice of a CEO. They did not ask any hard questions.

For the first couple of years, the board completed annual reviews with the CEO. Then the reviews stopped. Kent was doing so well that they seemed superfluous.

What were some of the warning signs that the board ignored? Here are a few:

- **Major programmatic changes.** The ministry programs were operating effectively before Kent became CEO. But in the first 12 months of his leadership, he made significant changes in the way the ministry delivered its programs. Some of these changes proved to be ineffective.

    ➢ *What the board missed:* They should have asked tough questions about the sudden and major program changes.

- **Significant staffing departures.** Within the first six months after Kent became the CEO, the ministry's chief financial officer, chief operating officer, and chief development officer resigned. The positions were filled with Kent's friends, all of whom turned out to be less effective than those who resigned.

    ➢ *What the board missed:* The sudden departure of highly valued staff members should have set off alarm bells.

- **Use of reserves.** The first few years of Kent's leadership were marked by operating losses and significant use of cash reserves. Kent explained away the losses, and the board accepted it.

➤ *What the board missed:* The board should have held Kent accountable to operate with revenue exceeding expenses.

- **Loss of major givers.** In the early years of Kent's leadership, there was a drip-drip-drip of major givers pulling back on their support of the ministry, and new givers were not identified to replace them.

  ➤ *What the board missed:* The board did not ask for or receive reports on the loss of major givers.

- **CEO reports to the board.** Kent's reports to the board— at board meetings and between meetings—became more generic over time, reflecting less innovation and less strategic thinking. There seemed to be a shift to less accountability and transparency in these reports.

  ➤ *What the board missed:* While the changes in Kent's reports were subtle, the changes in his accountability and transparency were obvious when viewed in the rearview mirror.

BOARDROOM LESSON

When cues and clues begin to accumulate,
a board should be very attentive to the possibility
of a falling CEO.

Board Action Steps:

○ 1. **Assess:** Conduct annual performance reviews of your CEO.

○ 2. **Partner:** Utilize a shared governance approach resulting in a strong partnership between your CEO and the board.

○ 3. **Watch:** Look for warning signs that your CEO is falling—and address them. (For a deeper dive on this topic, we highly recommend Chapter 8: "Spotting, Catching, or Exiting a Falling CEO" in *Boards That Lead* by Ram Charan, Dennis Carey, and Michael Useem.)

Prayer: "Lord, help our board to be properly attentive to the needs of our CEO—praying, encouraging, and monitoring progress. Amen."

27 | REPORT ONCE AND REPORT WITH CLARITY

Hearing the same report more than once is a "10" on the pain threshold!

Wasting the time of the board and board committees
with duplicative reporting
is inefficient and leads to boredom in the boardroom.

We had climbed onto the board reporting treadmill without recognizing it. There seemed to be no way to get off. It happened innocently enough.

We were a relatively small ministry with $2 million in annual revenue. In addition to an executive committee, an audit committee, and a governance committee, our board had a finance committee, a development committee, and a program committee. Every board member was on at least one committee, and some served on at least two. We routinely scheduled a full day prior to the board meeting just for the committees to meet.

We had an executive for each major area: finance, development, and program. So it only made sense that each executive should prepare a report for every board meeting, include it in the advance materials, and regurgitate the report in the respective committee meeting. After all, each committee needed to be regularly fed.

Perhaps your board does not have this many committees, so the excitement accompanying the double reporting all takes place at the board level.

Then, adding agony to frustration, the reports from the leadership team grew longer and longer, with few or no graphics. The reports were so voluminous that each board committee struggled to wade through them. Moreover, the details of these reports were totally lost on the board members who did not serve on the respective reporting committee. If the board ever did receive executive summaries, they were few and far between.

In her evaluation, Sally said the reports were poorly written in general, and the lack of summarization of the issues was especially troubling.

Our board did not have term limits, so it was a rare occurrence to see a new face at the board table. The board lifers never questioned the committee or reporting structure. The structure had become a way of life, so the process just rolled on and on.

Then one day, Ben passed away, leaving an open board seat. In due course, Sally was elected.

It was our custom for each board member to complete a one-page board evaluation after each meeting. The evaluations were summarized, and the results were provided to the board chair and the governance committee chair.

Sally, as a new board member, did not hold anything back. She was frustrated to the hilt. She had dutifully waded through all of the reports provided in the advance materials—

page by page, line by line, and word by word. In her evaluation, Sally said the reports were poorly written in general, and the lack of summarization of the issues was especially troubling.

Sally had been assigned to the development committee. So she asked the chief development officer to spend an hour explaining his report. Sally asked a few pertinent questions, and all were met with, "That is the way we have always done this," "You will understand this better after you have been on the board for a few years," and "Fundraising is too complex a topic for most board members to understand." Sally had some choice comments after this interchange.

How can a board like this improve? It may want to rethink the concept of term limits. It may want to reconsider the number of committees. Whether or not the board needs to address some of these issues peripheral to the reporting matter, here are some essential considerations:

- **Use executive summaries.** For every detailed report, there should be an executive summary that draws the attention of board members to the most salient information. Detailed reports can often be limited to three pages.

- **Report once.** If a board committee (or member of the executive team) has prepared a detailed written report for the board, the executive summary of the report can be summarized in a verbal report.

- **Use action-only reporting.** Consider submitting committee reports to the board only if there is potential action being recommended by a committee.

Effective reporting to the board is an art. It is rarely done with excellence. The tendency is to grovel in the humdrum instead of rising above the detail and reflecting on the big picture. Reporting once and reporting with clarity can keep the board out of the weeds and focused on the mission of the ministry.

BOARDROOM LESSON

How much is duplicative reporting costing your board?
Just place an hourly value on a board member's time,
multiply it by the number of board members,
and again by the number of reporting hours.

Board Action Steps:

○ 1. **Assess:** Review the current process and the extent of the reporting by staff to the board (see Lesson 36 for insights on heavy lifting).

○ 2. **Improve:** Determine how the process and reporting could be improved, then update appropriate sections of your Board Policies Manual (see Lesson 4).[1]

○ 3. **Change:** Commit to make the changes necessary to provide excellence in reporting to the board.

Prayer: Lord, help our staff to report what should be reported to the board and do it with such clarity that You are glorified. Amen."

PART 9:

HOLY GROUND
AND OTHER LOCATIONS

God said,
"Don't come any closer.
Remove your sandals from your feet.
You're standing on holy ground."

Exodus 3:5 (MSG)

28 | SLOW DOWN AND WAIT ON GOD

"He does not bestow his gifts on the casual or hasty."

> *God's acquaintance is not made hurriedly.*
> *He does not bestow His gifts*
> *on the casual or hasty comer and goer.*
> *To be much alone with God is the secret*
> *of knowing Him and of influence with Him.*[1]
>
> E. M. Bounds

Ruth Haley Barton puts a sharp stick into the heart of board decision-making that masquerades as discernment: "One very common leadership mistake is to think that we can take a group of undiscerning individuals and expect them to show up in a leadership setting and all of a sudden become discerning!"[2]

So how can boards do spiritual discernment together? How can boards invite the right people onto the board—individuals who have already demonstrated a competency in spiritual discernment?

Perhaps one question to ask board prospects is this: "In your own life, how do you spiritually discern God's voice?"

We know leaders who spend a day in prayer. We know boards and organizations that listen to God's voice during an annual day of prayer.

And while this is not prescriptive for every board or every board member, consider this wisdom from Lorne Sanny. In the following introduction to *How to Spend a Day in Prayer*, he shares the benefits of being in God's presence for an extended time of prayer. The introduction, reprinted with permission of NavPress (a ministry of The Navigators), continues through the end of this lesson.[3]

> "I never thought a day could make such a difference," a friend said to me. "My relationship to everyone seems improved."
>
> "Why don't I do it more often?"
>
> Comments like these come from those who set aside a personal Day of Prayer.
>
> With so many activities—important ones—clamoring for our time, real prayer is considered more a luxury than a necessity. How much more so spending a day in prayer!
>
> The Bible gives us three time-guides for personal prayer. There is the command to "pray without ceasing"—the spirit of prayer. Keeping so in tune with God that we can lift our hearts in request or praise anytime through the day.
>
> There is also the practice of a quiet time or morning watch—seen in the life of David (Psalm 5:3), of Daniel

(6:10), and of the Lord Jesus (Mark 1:35). This daily time specified for meditation in the Word of God and prayer is indispensable to the growing, healthy Christian.

Then there are examples in the Scripture of extended time given to prayer alone. Jesus spent whole nights praying. Nehemiah prayed "certain days" upon hearing of the plight of Jerusalem. Three times Moses spent 40 days and 40 nights alone with God.

Learning from God

I believe it was in these special times of prayer that God made known His ways and His plans to Moses (Psalm 103:7). He allowed Moses to look through a chink in the fence and gain special insights, while the rank-and-file Israelites saw only the acts of God as they unfolded day by day.

> *"During earlier years [Dawson Trotman] spent countless protracted time alone with God, and out of these times the Navigator work grew—not by methods or principles but by promises given to him from the Word."*

Once I remarked to Dawson Trotman, founder of The Navigators, "You impress me as one who feels he is a man of destiny, one destined to be used of God."

"I don't think that's the case," he replied, "but I know this. God has given me some promises that I know He will fulfill." During earlier years Dawson spent countless protracted time alone with God, and out of these times the Navigator work grew—not by methods or principles but by promises given to him from the Word.

In my own life one of the most refreshing and stabilizing factors, as well as the means for new direction or confirmation of the will of God, has been those extended times of prayer—in the neighborhood park in Seattle, on a hill behind the Navigator home in Southern California, or out in the Garden of the Gods here in Colorado Springs.

These special prayer times can become anchor points in your life, times when you "drive a stake" as a landmark and go on from there. Your daily quiet time is more effective as you pray into day-by-day reality some of the things the Lord speaks to your heart in protracted times of prayer. The quiet time, in turn, is the foundation for "praying without ceasing," going through the day in communion with God.

Perhaps you haven't spent a protracted time in prayer because you haven't recognized the need for it. Or maybe you aren't sure what you would do with a whole day on your hands just to pray.

Author's Note: After the introduction in Lorne Sanny's powerful 21-page booklet, he shares practical suggestions in six short sections: Why a Day of Prayer?, Pray on the Basis of God's Word, How to Go About It, Wait on the Lord, Prayer for Others, Prayer for Yourself, and Two Questions Answered. He adds:

The results of your day of prayer should be the answers to the two questions Paul asked on the Damascus road (Acts 9:5,6). His first question was "Who art Thou, Lord?" You will be seeking to know Him, to find out who He is. The second question, "Lord, what wilt Thou have me to do?" should be answered or reconfirmed in that part of the day when you unhurriedly seek His will for you.[4]

BOARDROOM LESSON

The busyness of life and governance to-do lists often create an environment that is not conducive to spiritually discerning God's voice about your ministry's future. Consider spending a day in prayer, by yourself, or as a board. Invite an experienced facilitator who will help your board slow down to discern direction.

Board Action Steps:

○ 1. **Read:** Here are three options: *How to Spend a Day in Prayer* by Lorne C. Sanny, *Strengthening the Soul of Your Leadership* by Ruth Haley Barton, and *Pursuing God's Will Together*, also by Ruth Haley Barton.

○ 2. **Retreat:** Consider a half-day retreat with your board. Use the *Spiritual Discernment Retreat Guide* by Stephen Macchia, which gives guidance for a half-day experience for individuals or groups (www.leadership transformations.org).

○ 3. **Rejuvenate:** Listen to the meditative praise song, "Slow Down" by Chuck Girard (Dunamis Music).

Prayer: "Lord, as Steve Macchia reminds us, 'Like many aspects of the spiritual life, discernment is hard to do on the run.' So it seems like a no-brainer to ask You, 'Should we spend a day in prayer?' Guide us. Amen."

29 | THINK AND PRAY OUTSIDE THE BOX— AND THE COUNTY

Discern your Big HOLY Audacious Goal (carefully).

Just because a goal is so big it can only be accomplished if God shows up does not mean it aligns with His will.[1]

Gary G. Hoag, R. Scott Rodin, and Wesley K. Willmer

Does your board need a kick in their, shall we say, vision?

Rather than enduring board meetings at the same-old-same-old locations with the same-old-same-old meals, plan a board meeting at an inspirational location.

Imagine if several decades ago, you had brought your board to New Life Ranch and heard Willard Heck's story about vision and God's faithfulness.[2]

In 1958, Heck and his partner bought almost a thousand acres in northeast Oklahoma and founded New Life Ranch, a nondenominational Christian camp. The audacity of his faith, like so many other founders, was extraordinary.

Leaders can lift a board's vision by reminding them of God's work in other locations. Not only do you need to think and pray outside the box, sometimes it helps to think outside the county. To inspire boards to imagine God's new story for them, I've shared the story that follows numerous times:

There I was in the middle of a tour of New Life Ranch and my eyes almost popped out upon seeing the camp's extensive, well-equipped bakery.

The bakery itself was larger than most camp kitchens! So I asked Willard Heck how he was able to afford such a huge kitchen, bakery, and dining hall. (You need to know that Heck, who was called to heaven in 2001, was as humble as he was filled with faith. I will never forget his simple response.)

Heck replied, "Well, I just showed the Lord our plans and blueprints for New Life Ranch and the kind of foodservice facilities we needed to do His work here. I told the Lord that if He was short of money, we could cut back on the plans. But if we were to create a facility and program that truly honored Him, then this is how much money we'd need. So the Lord provided the funds."

Contrast Heck's bold trust in the One Who owns the cattle on a thousand hills with the more frequent, sheepish response to Kingdom work: minimal, just-get-by, conservative, bargain basement. Willard Heck had his theology right and his prayer life tuned up for action.

Founders don't have a monopoly on faith and vision. Yet for CEOs and board members today, you'll need extraordinary faith to move your organization into the next ministry season. Ministry is hard work!

Decades back, it was often founders who inspired givers with raw land and radical plans. Today your board, perhaps, is faced with aging buildings, worn-out programs, demanding customers, and layers of bureaucracy. So how do we exercise our faith muscles?

King David gave Solomon the blueprints to the temple in 1 Chronicles 28:9, and urged him: "Get to know well your father's God" (MSG). Get to know Willard Heck's God. Get to know your founder's God.

"I told the Lord that if He was short of money, we could cut back on the plans. But if we were to create a facility and program that truly honored Him, then this is how much money we'd need. So the Lord provided the funds."

Then assemble your team, get on your knees, and discern His direction for the exciting years ahead. Resist the temptation to focus only on budgets, blueprints, and buildings. Instead, embrace those goals that focus on the people God is calling you to reach and serve.

Jim Collins, author of numerous helpful business books,[3] urges organizations to craft Big Hairy Audacious Goals (BHAGs). Ministry leaders might prefer to call them Big HOLY Audacious Goals. The classic BHAG: after Sputnik I orbited Earth in 1957, President Kennedy inspired the nation with this BHAG: "Put a man on the moon by 1970."

Some readers will remember where they were on July 20, 1969, when Neil Armstrong descended from Apollo 11 and walked on the moon. That was audacious!

BHAGs also bring out the best in givers. A few years ago, a ministry leader told me he challenged a giver to consider one of three projects: a $200,000 idea, a $300,000 program, or a $500,000 project. The giver's response? "Would it be okay if I funded all three?" That's Willard Heck faith.

At your next board retreat—on holy ground somewhere— celebrate the BHAGs of past decades and generations, but also take time to hear from God anew. Get to know the God of your founders. What is the Big HOLY Audacious Goal for five years from now that is a Willard Heck-type goal? What target is so big, so audacious, so needing the faith of zealots, that only God can deliver?

When you hear from God—and your staff and board hear from God—and you put that BHAG on the wall, it will energize and propel your ministry toward the future like nothing else. But consider also this caution, from the authors of *The Choice*: "Just because a goal is so big it can only be accomplished if God shows up does not mean it aligns with His will."[4]

Discern God's will for you. That's what Willard Heck did. Is it God's will for you to operate only year to year, with modest budget and program adjustments and without a compelling vision that is dependent on audacious faith? Is it God's will for you to lose momentum, miss Kingdom opportunities, and settle for second best, not God's best? Who signs up for that inaction plan?

BOARDROOM LESSON

Visit holy ground at other ministries
and learn about the faith and vision of their founders.
Leverage these inspirational settings with your board
to think, pray and discern God's direction for the future.

Board Action Steps:

○ 1. **Read:** Don't skim but dig deep into *The Choice: The Christ-Centered Pursuit of Kingdom Outcomes* by Gary G. Hoag, R. Scott Rodin, and Wesley K. Willmer.

○ 2. **Study:** Reflect on 1 Chronicles 28-29 and the strategic planning book built around this scripture: *Breakthrough: Unleashing the Power of a Proven Plan* by Randon A. Samelson.[5]

○ 3. **Visit:** Research an inspirational setting and story for your next board meeting.

Prayer: "Lord, we desire a ministry plan that is rooted in faithfulness-focused strategies and eternity-oriented metrics. Amen."

THE TRUCK DRIVER WAS NO MATCH FOR THE FAITH-FILLED BOARD CHAIR

Don't stop at "All in favor say aye."

> *I remember the story, perhaps apocryphal, about*
> *President Eisenhower and his secretary of state, John Foster Dulles.*
> *Dulles was an inveterate traveler. He seemed to be*
> *on the go continuously. At one point during the discussion*
> *of a serious problem, President Eisenhower said to him,*
> *"Don't just do something, stand there." Sometimes it's easier*
> *to be busy than to take the time to be reflective.*[1]
>
> Max De Pree

Picture this boardroom of faith-filled pioneers: Scandinavian Christ-followers who launched a Bible camp and conference center in the Seattle area in 1919.

As boards do sometimes, they saw a need, approved a motion, and adjourned the meeting. But days later, the need remained and the funding was still at zero.

In the first half of the twentieth century, men and women took on big challenges. Many board members were inspired by and recruited to Kingdom causes. Governance was important, but not as important as launching the programs and building the buildings.

"Welcome to the board. Please bring your hammers, saws, ladders, and backhoes."

Governance and planning back then had the flavor of Southwest Airlines founder Herb Kelleher, who said, "We have a 'strategic plan.' It's called doing things."[2]

So in that spirit and after that board meeting, Charlie Johnson ventured onto God's miracle stage. As board chair of Sammamish Bible Camp Association (later known as SAMBICA) in Bellevue, WA, Charlie was a man of action and a man of prayer. (That's a powerful combination!)

The board had done the easy part: approved the building of a tabernacle. Two problems though: summer was approaching, and no funds were available for this gathering place—potential holy ground for generations to come.

What to do? Charlie Johnson started with prayer. He returned to the quiet setting on Lake Sammamish and prayed and fasted for three days.

He asked God the Provider to allocate the resources for the tabernacle in time for the summer's harvest. (I'm thinking he meditated on Luke 12:24, "Consider the ravens…")

On that third day, according to the camp's 25th anniversary brochure, a large truck loaded with lumber drove onto the camp grounds. Johnson, a man of prayer and action, was ready for him.

> *He asked God the Provider to allocate the resources for the tabernacle in time for the summer's harvest.*

"You're the one the Lord has sent to build the tabernacle!"

The puzzled truck driver looked at Charlie and responded. "No, I'm just looking for an address near here. Can you help me?"

Imagine the verbal contest with this prayer warrior after three days of fasting! I'm guessing the driver was no match for the God-inspired faith of Charlie Johnson.

Impressed with this board chair's focused and faith-filled action plan, the driver conceded and began unloading the lumber. The historical account notes that following this defining moment, the tabernacle was built in just eight days.

Today, almost a hundred years later, SAMBICA continues to be holy ground for life-changing stories. Today, highly committed board members pray, steward, and act while fully cognizant of the spiritual heritage and legacy from a board chair who didn't stop at "All in favor say aye."

BOARDROOM LESSON

Sometimes what's missing is not the strategic plan, or the
capital campaign, or all the i's dotted and all the t's crossed.
What's missing is an encounter with God the Provider.
What's missing is a genuine heart to implement
His plan, not your plan.
What's missing is a compelling vision that is God-inspired.

Board Action Steps:

○ **1. Discuss:** If our board has perennial funding challenges,
could it be we are too busy implementing our plan and
not God's plan?

○ **2. Weigh:** Do we appropriately balance prayer and action?

○ **3. Reflect:** Do we function with a board mindset of
scarcity or abundance? For more insights, read *The
Sower: Redefining the Ministry of Raising Kingdom
Resources* by R. Scott Rodin and Gary G. Hoag.[3]

Prayer: "Lord, we confess to busyness over prayerfulness,
action over reflection, our wills over your will. We're sorry.
Help us listen and then act, but only when you speak. Amen."

PART 10:

BUILDING A 24/7 BOARD CULTURE

Integrity matters.
Strong and effective boards
intentionally engage in mutual accountability,
including systematic board development and evaluation.

In the long run, only integrity matters.
In fact, without integrity, there will be no long run.[1]

E. LeBron Fairbanks, Dwight M. Gunter II,
and James R. Couchenour

CUT THE CORD! INVITE BOARD MEMBERS 31 TO EXIT WHEN THEY DON'T LIVE YOUR VALUES

If you want a healthy board, recruit healthy people.

> *One of the myths of volunteer board work is that you see only fine, well-motivated people who agree on what needs to be done, when to do it, and how to do it. . . Good people disagree, do a little politicking, try to make decisions in the bathroom (the worst form of exclusion), and come to meetings totally unprepared.*[1]
>
> Max De Pree

I know. I know. It's so tempting to keep the peace and not deal with difficult or toxic board members. Take "George," for instance. He was in the second year of his three-year term. Yes, he created problems in virtually every board meeting, but hey—he'll term out in just five more board meetings. How bad can it be?

In an ECFA governance survey of more than 1,600 CEOs and board members of ECFA-accredited organizations, participants were asked to rate their boards against 20 effectiveness indicators. CEOs, board chairs, and board members all gave their lowest rating to this statement: "Our board has policies in place—and the spiritual integrity required—to ask an under-performing board member to resign."[2]

Governance takes guts! I learned this difficult boardroom lesson early in my CEO career. Our board's nominating committee was ready to enthusiastically recommend that a well-known person join our board.

Before the vote, a discerning board member asked a boardroom-silencing question: "Have you talked to his pastor recently?"

Of course, we hadn't. Long story short, the individual's lifestyle and values did not square with our board's values, and we went back to the recruitment drawing board. I should have thanked the board member for saving us a great deal of grief, but I was too embarrassed to bring it up again. Yikes.

The values discussion is mandatory. "One way to get a healthy culture is to hire healthy people," says Miles McPherson.[3]

So let me paraphrase McPherson: If you want a healthy board, recruit healthy people.

Jack and Suzy Welch describe "The Ultimate Values Test" in their book

> *If you want a healthy board, recruit healthy people.*

Winning: The Answers—Confronting 74 of the Toughest Questions in Business Today.[4] They list four kinds of managers in the typical organization or company. Perhaps your board includes all four types.

The Welches recommend that managers [and board members] should be evaluated on two key areas: their performance and how well they live out the corporate values. So for boards, two critical ingredients must be nailed down:

the board member's job description and your ministry's core values/corporate culture. Here's how I chart these insights:

THE ULTIMATE VALUES TEST		
Where are your board members today?	**LIVES OUR VALUES**	**DOES NOT LIVE OUR VALUES**
GREAT PERFORMANCE	**GROUP 1:** Praise and reward!	**GROUP 3:** Warning! Start walking the talk or you'll need to exit.
UNSATISFACTORY PERFORMANCE	**GROUP 2:** Give them another chance.	**GROUP 4:** Cut the cord!

To paraphrase Jack and Suzy Welch:

- **Board members in Group 1** deliver great results and adhere to your core values. "They should be praised and rewarded at every opportunity."

- **Board members in Group 2** deliver poor results but adhere to the values. They "deserve another chance, maybe in another position within the organization." Perhaps you'll need to give them a sabbatical from the board for a season—maybe inspiring them to serve in a volunteer role where they can have an impact.

- **Group 3 board members** deliver great results but don't live your values. In many organizations, says Welch, these people "deliver the numbers, but usually on the backs of their people. Companies very often keep these jerks around for way too long, destroying morale and trust as they do."

- **Board members in Group 4** have poor performance and poor values. This one's easy to deal with, says Welch. "When you finally get the guts to cut the cord, you'll wonder why you didn't do it sooner."

Welch also warns not to get rid of value offenders in Group 4 with surreptitious excuses such as, "Charles left for personal reasons to spend more time with his family." Instead, he cautions, inform your team publicly and "announce that Charles was asked to leave because he didn't adhere to specific company values."[5]

"One of the greatest gifts we can offer another person is a safe place to fail."[6] As you define and refine your board's core values, pray for a discerning spirit to know when you must show grace and when you must show someone the door.

BOARDROOM LESSON

When you have board members in Group 4
(not performing and not living the values),
invite them to exit the board.
Then, as you recruit new board members, remember this:
if you want a healthy board, recruit healthy people.

Board Action Steps:

○ **1. Delegate:** Invite a board member to read *Winning: The Answers* by Jack and Suzy Welch and then share several insights for the board at your next meeting.

○ **2. Review:** Dust off your bylaws and/or Board Policies Manual regarding the process for exiting a person from your board. Is the process clear?

○ **3. Inspire:** Share the four-group chart at your next board meeting and inspire board members to function at a high level as Group 1 members.

Prayer: "Lord, help me to walk the talk 24/7 and also as a board member—in and out of board meetings. Amen."

32 | LOOSE LIPS SINK THE BOARDROOM SHIP

What happens in the boardroom must stay in the boardroom.

*Board members who leak confidential information
about the ministry they serve
disqualify themselves from board service—period!*

Gil seemed to be such a good board member. He attended all board meetings and he was thoroughly prepared. His comments in the boardroom were especially insightful. He helped identify potential financial supporters for the ministry. He was a model board member, but…

Gil had an Achilles heel. He had loose lips. When visiting with non-board members, he frequently shared what was happening at the ministry. This would have been fine had he not gone beyond information that was publicly available.

In Gil's first board meeting, the board discussed an incident of fraud that occurred within the ministry. The matter had not been reported in the media. A few days after the meeting, Gil mentioned the fraud to some friends at his church.

Then, in Gil's second board meeting, the board discussed a moral failure by one of the ministry's executives. Again, the matter was not publicly known. Soon after the board meeting,

Gil shared the confidential information he had learned in the board meeting with some of his business colleagues.

No one knew Gil's motives. However, it appeared he had a personal need to be the first to release insider information, hoping to gain personal importance by doing so.

Sadly, just the opposite occurred. Gil's friends and colleagues were shocked that he felt comfortable sharing information that a board member should have kept under wraps.

It is impossible to over-estimate the importance of keeping confidences as a board member. The results of a board member with loose lips include the following:

At least annually, board members should be required to provide a written acknowledgment of the confidentiality policy and their commitment to abide by the policy.

- **Loss of personal respect.** While a few people may be impressed when a ministry board member leaks confidential information, most folks will see it for what it is: inappropriate sharing of information. The end result almost always will be a loss of personal respect for the loose-lipped board member coupled with wonderment as to how the individual was ever qualified to serve on the board.

- **Loss of ministry respect.** While the board member leaking information may not think his or her actions will harm the ministry, it often does exactly that. Some leaked information may have otherwise never been made public.

What should boards do to protect confidential information? The remedy is simple and straight-forward:

1. **Establish a sound board policy.** Start with a board policy that addresses confidentiality guidelines and delineates who speaks for the board. Generally, this is limited to the CEO (and his or her designee) and the board chair. The policy should prohibit disclosure of information about the ministry's activities unless the board and/or ministry decides to make the information public, or unless the information is a matter of public record. At least annually, board members should be required to provide a written acknowledgment of the confidentiality policy and their commitment to abide by the policy.

2. **Blow the whistle early.** There is often a tendency not to address the lack of confidentiality because of the collegiality of board members. When it is first determined that a board member has violated the privacy policy, the issue must be brought to the board chair's attention. Otherwise, a confidentiality policy is meaningless.

3. **Directly address the matter with the board member.** The board chair and/or the governance committee (or similar committee) chair should privately consult with the board member.

4. **Extend grace for the first offense.** If the matter can be settled in a private meeting—and the offending board member admits the indiscretion and commits to never repeat the offense—perhaps the matter need not be brought to the full board.

5. **Follow the two strikes rule.** In baseball, a batter gets three strikes before they are out. When a board member leaks confidential information and it has been highlighted with the member, the second offense should be the end of the line. Ensure that your bylaws or Board Policies Manual addresses the process for asking a board member to resign. Then, if permitted, ask for the board member's resignation following the appropriate guidelines.

Few things can destroy the trust of a ministry and its board as quickly as when a board member leaks confidential information. Though this may be the way of life in some corners of the secular world and with governmental officials, this is God's work, and we are called to a much higher standard.

BOARDROOM LESSON

A key responsibility of every board member
is to unequivocally honor the confidentiality
of what is said in the boardroom.
However, confidentiality does not stop
with the boardroom; it extends to any non-public
information that a board member learns based
on his or her board involvement.
There are no exceptions.

Board Action Steps:

○ 1. **Write:** Start with a clear board privacy policy that spells out confidentiality requirements in detail, and include the policy in the Board Policies Manual (see Lesson 4).[1]

○ 2. **Sign:** To serve as an important reminder, the board should sign a confidentiality statement at least annually.

○ 3. **Abide:** If any board member is aware of a breach of the confidentiality policy, the board chair should immediately be notified. The board chair should then privately meet with the offending board member to determine if this will be an ongoing pattern or if the board member is willing to abide by the privacy policy.

Prayer: "Lord, help each board member to maintain a protocol of strict confidentiality concerning what is said in the boardroom, even if it doesn't seem that sharing information will cause any harm. Amen."

33 | "GOOD IS THE ENEMY OF GREAT"

When great board experiences end, they should be lamented.

> *Greatness is an inherently dynamic process, not an end point.*
> *The moment you think of yourself as great,*
> *your slide toward mediocrity will have already begun.*[1]
>
> Jim Collins

Many board experiences are good for the board member and the board. Few are great experiences, in a large part because it is so easy to settle for good experiences. As Jim Collins says, "Good is the enemy of great."[2]

The goal for every ministry should be to create great board experiences for every board member. While *good* board experiences are par for the course, boards have a higher calling. And when a *great* board member terms off your board, take time to honor how that person has enriched your lives and the effectiveness of your ministry. And it is appropriate for a board member to lament leaving a great board.

The difference between good and great board experiences is larger than one would imagine.

Tom completed six years of service on a ministry board. He left the board only because he reached the term limit imposed by the bylaws. Tom believed he had a great board experience. David, the ministry's CEO, agreed.

Because great board experiences are not commonplace, I spoke to both Tom and David to gain insights into what made this a great experience all the way around. Here is what David observed about Tom:

- **Unfazed by challenges.** The ministry faced some unusually strong challenges during Tom's board tenure. David said that Tom was not fazed by the challenges. Tom could be counted on to thoughtfully consider even the most difficult issues and support sound recommendations.

- **Unwavering support.** While the board was generally supportive of its CEO, David had a special sense that he could always count on Tom for support when the going got tough.

  When term limits mandate that you bid farewell to a great board member, take time to honor how that person has enriched your lives and the effectiveness of your ministry.

- **Shared influence.** Tom was generous in sharing his important connections with David and the ministry. Every board member has connections that are helpful to the ministry they serve; it is the sharing of those connections that is the key.

- **Creative thought.** When outside-the-box thinking was helpful, Tom came through every time. Tom was all about clock building, not time telling.

- **Generosity of time.** Tom not only made board meeting attendance a priority, he was generous in his time in serving on board committees.

And here is how Tom characterized his time on the board:

- **Connection with an organization of significance.** Tom found it rewarding to allocate his time, energy, and bandwidth to this ministry that shone Kingdom light in a corner of the world that needs that light. We live in a broken world, and the role of a ministry board is to bring wholeness to that brokenness. Tom believed this ministry made a Kingdom difference.

- **Wrestling with real issues that require wisdom.** Tom knew that to do a good job you need to *have* a good job. That is true in actual job positions (for-profit and nonprofit) as well as in board positions (for-profit and nonprofit). Tom recognized the huge difference between problems that require solutions and reports that invite feedback. It is a waste of resources to gather a high-horsepower board to simply listen to reports.

- **Membership in a well-constructed board community.** Tom appreciated the board chemistry. Achieving the right chemistry—the right tone and tenor of a group that works well together is harder than it looks. It is possible to have very good people on the board, but who don't mesh well together and that impacts good governance. It is also possible to have very good chemistry, but without effective governance. Tom noted that the best boards have both.

- **Robust interaction in a space of guaranteed confidentiality.** Tom said this was a great board experience because it had both "robust interaction" and "guaranteed confidentiality." Robust interaction assumes that the board is not simply a rubber stamp of management decisions, and/or that the board's wisdom is needed and valuable. If confidentiality is not guaranteed—or is assured but ends up being breached—then the necessary interaction is muted.

BOARDROOM LESSON

The goal for every ministry should be to create great board experiences for every board member. While *good* board experiences are par for the course, boards have a higher calling.

Board Action Steps:

○ **1. Assess:** Take inventory of the quality of the board experience offered by your ministry.

○ **2. Improve:** Determine how the quality of the board experience can be significantly improved. (Ask board members for input, and always conduct an exit interview when board members term off the board.)

○ **3. Implement:** Design the necessary steps to achieve the identified improvements.

Prayer: "Lord, help us to create a board atmosphere conducive to *great* board experiences. Amen."

PART 11:

BOARDS THAT LEAD
AND BOARDS THAT READ

Leaders have a responsibility before God
to *constantly* get better,
and one of the most reliable ways to do so is to read.
Great leaders read frequently. They read voraciously.
They read classics and new releases.
They soak up lessons from the military,
from academia, from politics,
from nongovernmental organizations,
and from church leaders who are leading well.
They refuse to let themselves off the hook in this regard,
because they know that all great leaders read.[1]

Bill Hybels

34 | ENVISION YOUR BEST BOARD MEMBER ORIENTATION EVER

Equip new board members to serve from day one.

> *The author—a friend of mine—often jokes*
> *that a greeter at Walmart gets more orientation*
> *than most board members ever do. We all know that's no joke.*
> *It's true for boards of every description. And it is appalling.*[1]
>
> Patrick Lencioni

Jay joined the ministry board. His only board experience was serving on for-profit boards and his church board. Neither service provided him with a good background for service on this board.

He expected to receive a board orientation but never did. He was welcomed at his first board meeting. The board chair said it would be easy for him to catch up to the board's style of governance. In other words, the board tossed Jay into the deep end. After serving for two years, he began to understand the ministry and what serving on this board was all about.

Contrast this with Becky, who joined another ministry board. Once she was elected to the board, she received a thorough electronic binder of background materials. Prior to her first meeting, the board chair, the governance committee chair, and the CEO conducted a two-hour orientation with her explaining key ministry information and sharing the inner workings of the board. She had an opportunity to ask background questions. With her learning curve shortened, Becky felt well prepared to be an active and productive board member at her very first meeting.

Orientation of new board members is one of the most neglected aspects of board governance. Many ministries don't do it at all, leaving their board members to wing it.[2] The quality of the orientation process is a reflection of the quality of the board and the ministry.

A solid orientation begins at the pre-election point. This is when a prospective board member is provided information on the history, mission, and culture of your ministry.

The more rigorous orientation begins post-election but before the new member's first board meeting. This process requires scheduling, planning, and thoughtful execution. If more than one new board member is joining the board at the same time, perhaps a joint meeting can be arranged for time efficiency.

> *Orientation of new board members is one of the most neglected aspects of board governance. The quality of the orientation process is a reflection of the quality of the board and the ministry.*

For local boards, there is often more flexibility in scheduling an in-person meeting with the board chair, CEO, and board governance chair. Larger ministries may want to include the chief operating officer, chief financial officer, and chief development officer in the meeting. For boards with members from across a region, the United States, or the world, the orientation may immediately precede their first board meeting or be conducted electronically.

What are the elements of a first-class board member orientation? Here are the basics:

A. History of the ministry

B. Mission, Vision, and Core Values statements

C. Update on major trends by ministry segment

D. Basic board information

    a. Board member bios

    b. Board committee members and charters

    c. Ministry bylaws

    d. Board meeting minutes—for at least the previous 12 months

    e. Summary of directors' and officers' insurance coverage

    f. Board Policies Manual

    g. Board member duties and responsibilities including:

        a) Conflict of interest policy

        b) Confidentiality policy

    h. Board travel reimbursement policy

    i. Calendar of meetings for at least the next two years

E. Financial information and IRS filings

    a. Most recent budget

    b. Most recent interim financial reports

    c. Most recent yearend financial reports

    d. Most recent Form 990, if applicable

F. Strategic plan

    a. Current and multi-year plan

    b. Program overview

G. Key dashboard indicators and metrics—financial and programmatic

H. Key organizational information

    a. Ministry's major programs and services. If the organization provides services internationally, provide an overview of such programs, including how the ministry provides oversight of services carried out.

    b. Resource development plan and opportunities or expectations for board member participation

    c. Organizational chart

    d. Key staff position descriptions

    e. Key staff member bios

I. Tour of the facilities, if appropriate

J. Question and answer session

The point of an outstanding board member orientation
process is to:

- Prepare a board member to productively serve from day
  one.

- Inform the new member about their role and how the
  ministry operates.

- Make the board member proud of their new role and be
  able to share a few accomplishments of the ministry with
  family, friends, and colleagues.

- Help the new member feel valued and appreciated.

When you build a powerful orientation process into your
board member recruitment process, you will be equipping
new board members to serve with confidence from day one.

BOARDROOM LESSON

It is difficult to overestimate the importance
of a quality orientation process for new board members.
Failure to do so disrespects the value of the new members
and discredits the board and the ministry.

Board Action Steps:

○ 1. **Assess:** Evaluate your ministry's current orientation
process for new board members.

○ 2. **Improve:** Determine how the board member
orientation process can be improved. View the *ECFA
Governance Toolbox Series No. 1: Recruiting Board
Members.*[3]

○ 3. **Implement:** Take immediate steps to improve the
orientation process.

Prayer: "Lord, may we be good stewards of the service of new
board members, preparing them to make positive contributions from day one of their board service. Amen."

35 | IS YOUR BOARD COLOR-BLIND?

What color is your boardroom flag?

*Our board was lulled into complacency
and did not recognize the flag flying in the board room.
We thought the flags were green long after they had turned to yellow.*

Living near Indianapolis for several years, I occasionally stopped by the Indianapolis Motor Speedway, also known as the Brickyard.

At race tracks, flags are used to indicate track conditions and communicate important messages to drivers. The starter waves the flags atop a flag stand near the start/finish line.

The solid green flag is waved by the official to start the race. During a race, it is displayed at the end of a caution period or temporary delay to indicate that the race is restarting.

The solid yellow flag, or caution flag, requires drivers to slow down due to a hazard on the track—typically an accident, a stopped car, debris, or light rain.

The solid red flag is displayed when conditions are too dangerous to continue the race.

In every board meeting, there are flags that fly—green, yellow, or red—corresponding to the current atmosphere in the boardroom. The color of the flags can go through the entire spectrum in one meeting. In some cases, a flag of one color may fly for the entire meeting or most of it.

Hopefully, every board meeting starts out with a green flag flying. However, a red flag may have been flying at the end of the last board meeting, and there could be a carryover impact on the current meeting.

Does your board recognize the color of the flag flying in the boardroom, or is the board color-blind? Boards that know the color of the flag are in a position to more readily address issues that may cause "hazardous conditions."

Here are two examples of yellow and red flags:

- **Too much intensity.** The boardroom discussion begins positively; great input and collegiality—green flag. Then a new topic is introduced, and there is passionate discussion. Suddenly passion turns to intensity—too much intensity— yellow flag. Intensity changes to some harsh words between two board members—red flag.

  Recognizing the change in the flags during this discussion can help the board chair diffuse an otherwise ugly situation.

- **Too little intensity.** You have likely attended a board meeting that suffered from boredom. There was little engagement by the board—the board members were simply going through the motions. Some members were texting; others were answering emails. It was a yellow-flag meeting from start to finish.

- **Financial concerns.** A minor deficit for one year probably doesn't even rate a yellow flag. However, a large annual deficit qualifies for at least a yellow flag, and the larger it is, the more likely it is to become a red flag.

Here is a principle you can depend on: Yellow flags are on the income statement. Red flags are on the balance sheet.

Here is a principle you can depend on: Yellow flags are on the income statement. Red flags are on the balance sheet.

Boards that focus too much of their attention on the income statement may miss the red flags on the balance sheet.

There are hundreds of reasons why boards miss the color of the flags in the boardroom. These include disengaged boards, weak fiscal controls, misunderstanding of roles and responsibilities, and lack of timely information. More frequently, boards are just unaware of the three colored flags—and what they mean.

BOARDROOM LESSON

In every board meeting, there are flags that fly—green, yellow, or red. We can dream of seeing only green flags in each board meeting. However, the reality is that yellow flags often fly, and once in a while, you will see a red flag. Boards that recognize the color of the flags are in a better position to navigate thorny issues.

Board Action Steps:

○ 1. **Rate:** How would you rate the sensitivity of your board to observing the colors of flags in the boardroom? If the rating isn't high, determine to increase the board's sensitivity quotient.

○ 2. **Recognize:** Commit to discerning the color of the flags that are flying in future board meetings.[1]

○ 3. **Reflect:** At the end of each board meeting, assess how the board is doing in its sensitivity to the color of boardroom flags.

Prayer: "Lord, help our board to be sensitive to the boardroom atmosphere and the color of the flags that are flying. Amen."

36 DECREASE STAFF REPORTING AND INCREASE HEAVY LIFTING

Consider the good, the bad, and the ugly.

> *You start by introducing your topic.*
> *Then you say, "If I were you, I'd ask three questions about this topic."*
> *Write the questions on a flip chart.*
> *Answer the three questions. Then stop.*[1]
>
> Joey Asher

Like you, we've observed and endured our fair share of staff reports at board meetings. The most common sins follow this routine:

- The five direct reports to the CEO prepare single-spaced monthly reports (two to three pages each).

- The narratives (maybe with a few numbers) describe the last 30 days and are activity oriented, not results focused.

- Reports rarely mention a team member's progress on the three to five annual SMART goals (Specific, Measurable, Achievable, Realistic, Time-driven) because goals for the team (and the CEO) are not part of the culture.

- Then each team member reads the same report at the board meeting—the worst sin of all.

Staff reports, in our experience, fit into three categories: the Good, the Bad, and the Ugly. We'll start with the ugly so we end on a high note.

THE UGLY

The Problem: Ill-prepared and unrehearsed, some senior staff see a verbal board report as their opportunity to dazzle the board should the CEO be downed by the proverbial bus. It's all too obvious and frequently cringe-worthy. The "ugly" reports are rarely short and pithy—or helpful to the board's role. They often regurgitate written reports that many board members stopped reading years ago.

The Solution: CEOs must coach senior staff so their reports are humble, accurate, and related to board policy at the highest level. When staff misunderstand the role of the board and the proper role of staff reports at the board meeting, it's often too tempting for board members to inappropriately engage and micromanage the tantalizing topics served up by staff. The board chair must nip this in the bud!

Every report-giver should read *15 Minutes Including Q&A: A Plan to Save the World from Lousy Presentations* by Joey Asher. The book's very first paragraph is your red flag:

> Most business presentations stink. Really stink. They stink in a way that drains souls. They stink in a way that makes people think to themselves, "I flew in from LA for this? Maybe my mom was right. Maybe I should have gone to medical school."[2]

THE BAD

The Problem: Even with a well-coached staff member who understands where the board has landed on the policy governance continuum, bad things do happen—and it's often spelled "PowerPoint."

The Solution: Board guru Eugene H. Fram preaches, "The maximum number of slides in a PowerPoint presentation is ten." (Asher says six.) Fram's book *Going for Impact* has nine more rules in the short chapter "How to Use Board Members' Time Wisely."[3]

> *[They] …allocate one to two hours at each quarterly board meeting for what they call "heavy lifting." Here the board practices generative thinking and wrestles with a big ministry opportunity or dilemma.*

Balance the ten-slide edict with the social styles of your board members.[4] Analyticals thrive on data. Drivers prefer just five slides. Amiables would enjoy PowerPoints with relationship stories and photos. And you'll bless Expressives by inserting photos of them!

THE GOOD

The Problem: You'd think board members would appreciate a buttoned-down, quick staff presentation on the 2020 Vision Project: on schedule, under budget, high customer satisfaction ratings, and powerful Kingdom impact. No problems! That's always good news, but remember this: board members need to be needed.

Even when delivering excellent reports, the CEO and staff must discern how to engage board members and inspire their best thinking and discernment. (See Lesson 14.)

The Solution: Ed McDowell, executive director at Warm Beach Camp and Conference Center in Stanwood, WA, works with his board chair to allocate one to two hours at each quarterly board meeting for what they call "heavy lifting." Here the board practices generative thinking and wrestles with a big ministry opportunity or dilemma.

In response to CEO and staff reports, big issues, and opportunities, boards should pray, discern, and welcome conflicting views. And (*this really happens!*) they drive home from those meetings with a holy sense that they were needed, and each oar in the water actually mattered!

BOARDROOM LESSON

Encourage your CEO to coach all senior team members prior to every board meeting on the role of the board (usually policy, not down-in-the-weeds) and the opportunity to engage the board in heavy lifting—board-level matters that need their wisdom, spiritual discernment, and hearts.

Board Action Steps:

○ 1. **Recommend:** Encourage your CEO and every person who gives board reports to read *15 Minutes Including Q&A* by Joey Asher.

○ 2. **Test:** For the next two meetings, test a rule that no presentation may have more than ten PowerPoint slides.

○ 3. **Pray:** The next time all of your CEO's senior staff are scheduled to be in the boardroom, create a memorable time of prayer and affirmation. In advance, for example, arrange for five board members to pray for the five team members. Perhaps give team members a specially selected Scripture verse for their desks as a reminder that the board has their back!

Prayer: "Lord, as board members, we don't do the work. We are dependent on our CEO and team members who do the work. Give them wisdom as they report and give us discernment as we wrestle with those heavy lifting agenda items. Amen."

37 | DON'T STRETCH CREDULITY WITH BHAGS AND STRETCH GOALS

The actual achievement of audacious goals is very uncommon.

Most chief executives are constitutionally optimistic,
and since by definition their role is to surmount challenges,
the tenor they bring into the boardroom
is likely to be relentlessly upbeat.[1]

Ram Charan, Dennis Carey, and Michael Useem

Remember Stretch Armstrong? "Stretch" was one of my son's favorite toys. The well-muscled blonde man's most notable feature: he could be stretched from his original size of about 15 inches to four or five feet!

Has Stretch Armstrong appeared in your boardroom? Maybe not, but you've likely discussed stretch goals and audacious targets. Perhaps stretch goals are already a proud feature of your current strategic plan.

Daring goals are often used to motivate staff. Google has long promoted the stretch goals philosophy, noting "More often than not, [daring] goals can tend to attract the best people and create the most exciting work environments....stretch goals are the building blocks for remarkable achievements in the long term."[2]

So it's no wonder that some ministries employ stretch goals as a magical formula to "resuscitate or transform an ailing" strategy.[3]

Stretch goals are often misunderstood. Stretch goals are not merely challenging goals, which are sometimes referred to by ministries as Big Holy Audacious Goals (BHAGs).[4] Stretch goals are nearly impossible goals often proposed by the CEO—like a moon shot. But beware! Even with solid faith in God's power, stretch goals fall into the miracle category.

So it's no wonder that some ministries employ stretch goals as a magical formula to "resuscitate or transform an ailing" strategy.

For example, at your next board meeting, your CEO proposes a strategic plan that would increase the ministry's annual revenue by 15 to 20 percent. That might qualify as a BHAG if God is in it.

But suppose the CEO proposes a strategic plan to increase the ministry's annual revenue by 40 percent or more. That is a stretch goal, and the board and CEO should admit it is a radical expectation!

As we've observed in hundreds and hundreds of ministries over the years, the numbers reveal the reality. Successfully achieving stretch goals is very uncommon, and thus reaching for the moon (and beyond!) should generally be avoided.

When should boards veto stretch goals? Here are three cautionary situations:

1. **The new CEO.** When a new CEO accepts the leadership baton of a ministry, there is often a desire to quickly make a strong impression. Therefore, it is not unusual for the CEO to recommend a stretch goal that verges on the unreasonable. And since the new leader is usually in a honeymoon period, the board may be prone to approve an unrealistic stretch goal. *Danger ahead!*

2. **The failing ministry.** When a ministry has experienced a negative multiyear track record with severe resource constraints and a loss of momentum, a stretch goal should rarely be used. Stabilization should generally be the goal for a ministry on a downward slide. A ministry that goes for broke with no capacity to actually execute a plan might get what they wish for—*broke!*

3. **The legacy-prone CEO.** When a CEO is in the last few years before retirement, there can be a temptation to adopt a fly-to-the-sun approach in an effort to cement the CEO's legacy. (Yes, even ministry leaders have egos.) Instead, the board should focus on a smooth transition between leaders as the primary goal. Stretch goals are rarely appropriate in the last few years of a CEO's tenure. *Legacy endangered!*

Stretch goals may be the ticket in somewhat rare situations. But before your board approves a fly-to-the-moon strategic plan, be sure your ministry is in step with God's leading.

As Ruth Haley Barton notes, "Just because something is strategic does not necessarily mean it is God's will for us right now."[5]

BOARDROOM LESSON

If your CEO is tempted to shoot for the moon, beware!
This may not be the right time to attempt
a Big Holy Audacious Goal or an unrealistic stretch goal.

Board Action Steps:

○ 1. **Reflect:** Encourage your board to read "The Stretch Goal Paradox" (*Harvard Business Review*, January-February, 2017).

○ 2. **Review:** Assess the goal-setting process in place for your ministry. Were last year's goals achieved? Are your proposed goals too audacious or too timid? Are they holy?

○ 3. **Discern:** Pray and discern how goals should be set, especially in three situations: a new CEO, a declining ministry track record, and a CEO near retirement.

Prayer: "Lord, help us to understand the difference between setting challenging goals versus setting nearly *impossible* goals. Amen."

38 GREAT BOARDS DELEGATE THEIR READING

Deputize a "Leaders Are Readers Champion."

If you were marooned on a desert island and
could have only a single book with you, what would you choose?
Somebody once asked this question of G. K. Chesterton.
Given his reputation as one of the most erudite and creative
Christian writers in the first half of the twentieth Christian century,
one would naturally expect his response to be the Bible. It was not.
Chesterton chose Thomas' Guide to Practical Shipbuilding.[1]

John Ortberg

I was shocked—but pleasantly shocked.

At a coffee break in a two-day board enrichment workshop, a lifelong learning CEO asked me to recommend "the best governance book" his board should read. So we strolled over to the resource table, and I began my lecture.

Me: Actually, there is no one perfect book for every board. It depends on many factors: previous board experience (the good kind!), your board's operating philosophy (the continuum from Policy Governance® to hands-on boards), your board's competencies in ten or more traditional roles and responsibilities . . .

He interrupted. Apparently, I was preaching, not helping.

CEO: Yeah. I get all that. But what do *you* recommend?

Me: Okay. But are you looking for a faith-based governance book or wanting to address any specific issue or opportunity? For example, here's a really good one: *Owning Up: The 14 Questions Every Board Member Needs to Ask* by Ram Charan. I especially appreciate how boards must wrestle with the question "Does the board own the strategy?"

CEO: We've already read that. Great book!

Me: Way to go! Then how about this one: *The Imperfect Board Member: Discovering the Seven Disciplines of Governance Excellence* by Jim Brown. It's not faith-based, but the author is a Christian—and get this—the board expert in this Patrick Lencioni-type business fable is a pastor!

CEO: We read it!

Me: What is this, a quiz show? Wow! Your board is well read. How about this one: *Best Practices for Effective Boards* by Fairbanks, Gunter, and Couchenour?

Finally I pitched a book that his board had not read. I also mentioned several more, including the *Harvard Business Review* article "What Makes Great Boards Great," by Jeffrey Sonnenfeld.[2] The author explains it's not rules and regulations— it's the way people work together—that creates a great board.

We've observed that there are several best practices that learning boards embrace:

- **Learning boards feature brief book reviews at every board meeting.** Great boards delegate their reading. Every board member doesn't need to read every governance book. However, with advance planning and motivation, the board chair can inspire individual board members to read and report on a helpful governance book. Some boards set a timer on the book reviewer for four or five minutes. If the reviewer concludes the report before the bell rings, he or she earns a Starbucks card!

  Appoint one board member to keep the "leaders are readers" core value on the front burner.

- **Learning boards inspire everyone to read the same book prior to the annual board retreat.** Select one stimulating book for everyone to read and include a "Read and Reflect Worksheet." Provide three options: Good—read five chapters; Better—read eight chapters; Best—read every chapter. Invite selected board members to share four-minute reviews of their assigned chapters. You'll be amazed at the preparation! No one wants to be remembered as the unprepared presenter.

- **Learning boards deputize a "Leaders Are Readers Champion."** Appoint one board member to keep the "leaders are readers" core value on the front burner. Provide a small budget so he or she can keep abreast of the latest trends, resources, training, books, blogs, videos, toolboxes, and websites that will help your board be lifelong learners.

So what is "the best governance book" your board should read next? It depends, of course, on your unique situation. As you spiritually discern God's direction for your ministry, your journey can be enhanced by the books you read (or listen to). Inspire your board to read!

BOARDROOM LESSON

Appoint an avid reader on your board as your "Leaders Are Readers Champion." Provide a small budget, and inspire your champion to keep lifelong governance learning top of mind for all board members.

Board Action Steps:

○ **1. Appoint**: Inspire a board member (perhaps a member of your governance committee) to be your "Leaders Are Readers Champion" with a brief focus on governance at each board meeting. (See Lesson 39.)

○ **2. Review:** Keep a running list of books and resources that the board has read in recent years, and inspire new board members to become familiar with the key concepts.

○ **3. Read!** Don't just talk about reading—do it!

Prayer: "Lord, many of us have experienced profound personal insights by reading the right book at the right time. Some of us have even made life-altering decisions after reading significant books. So guide us in our selection of books. Amen."

39 | INVEST "10 MINUTES FOR GOVERNANCE" IN EVERY BOARD MEETING

We are all guilty of bringing our delightful dysfunctions into every new board experience.

Leadership is a complex field and no one resource can meet all the needs of every leader in every situation.[1]

Richard Kriegbaum

During the same week I was writing this chapter, I helped facilitate a two-day learning experience for board members and CEOs from 11 nonprofit ministries. One board member—very astute, with excellent questions—cornered me at a coffee break.

"Whew! I have served on numerous boards," he confessed, "but I had no idea—no idea!—how much more is involved in board governance. The literature. The resources. The various models of governance. In the first two hours of our sessions, I realized I have so much to learn!"

That's a common response from board members who take the time to become better stewards of God's work.

The typical boardroom includes a mix of new and long-term board members who bring their previous board experiences (or lack of experiences) into your boardroom. Every board member carries unhealthy baggage into your meeting that passed as normalcy in a previous boardroom.

We are all guilty of bringing our delightful dysfunctions into every new board experience:

- Jennifer's previous board was inundated with board reports, but not until the morning of the board meeting. She was lulled into believing that the last-minute deluge of documents was acceptable.

- Enrique served on a board that rarely had a quorum present, so he tilts towards grace over policy.

- Alex was shocked to find his current board spends most of its precious time in the management weeds, with nary a dashboard in sight. His previous board— thanks to dashboards— measured and monitored progress thoughtfully and quickly.

> *The number of years served on boards may not be a good indicator of meaningful board experience. That's why board members must be lifelong learners.*

So how do you bring a diverse group of people together— and point them down the appropriate governance highway meeting after meeting after meeting?

The number of years served on boards may not be a good indicator of meaningful board experience. That's why board members must be lifelong learners. That's why many boards enhance the board member experience by featuring a "10 Minutes for Governance" segment in every meeting.

The big idea: In every board meeting, we want to remind board members that good governance does not happen by osmosis. It happens only with intentionality, training, and keeping critical governance topics (like focusing on policy, not operations) on everyone's radar.

To get started, create a master list of possible topics (board policies, recruiting board members, understanding financial reports, ten basic responsibilities of nonprofit boards, the distinctives of Christ-centered governance, etc.). You might also find helpful topics using selected chapters from this book.

Here are some specific examples of "10 Minutes for Governance" topics I've observed in boardrooms:

- **"Balancing Board Roles—The Three Hats: Governance, Volunteer, and Participant."** One board showed the short video from the ECFA Governance Toolbox Series.[2]

- **"Board Members as Lifelong Learners."** A board member featured insights from Chapter 68: "Read All You Can" in *Leadership Axioms* by Bill Hybels.[3]

- **"Ten Listening Guidelines to Improve Boardroom Communication."** This segment featured Ruth Haley Barton's thoughts on "entering into and maintaining a listening posture that helps us hear and interact in ways that are most fruitful."[4] See Lesson 18.

- **"Rules of the Road for Christlike Conflict Management."**
  Read this excellent two-page list in *Best Practices for
  Effective Boards.*[5]

Teachers often learn more than their students, so rotate the
leadership of this segment. Give board members advance
notice when asking them to prepare a presentation. Suggest
that each ten-minute segment include at least four to five
minutes of interaction and dialogue. *Example:* "In groups of
two, read these ten listening guidelines and identify the one
guideline that is most difficult for you." (Use a timer that
buzzes at ten minutes.)

In addition to assigned reading prior to board retreats, and
inspiring board members to read at least one governance
book a year, you'll discover that a "10 Minutes for
Governance" segment at every meeting will keep Christ-
centered governance on the front burner.

> Watch for the next book in this series,
> *More Lessons From the Nonprofit Boardroom,*
> with more practical take-aways for your
> "10 Minutes for Governance" segment in
> every board meeting.

BOARDROOM LESSON

To get alignment with both new and longtime board members, begin board meetings with a 10-minute segment on good governance. You'll have less conflict over competing governance models and more joy as you pursue Christ-centered governance.

Board Action Steps:

○ 1. **Read:** "An intelligent person is always eager to take in more truth, fools feed on fast-food fads and fancies." (Proverbs 15:14 MSG)

○ 2. **Focus:** Are board members inspired by the unique distinctives and benefits of Christ-centered governance versus secular governance models? Address that opportunity at least once a year in the "10 Minutes for Governance" segment.

○ 3. **Evaluate:** Are some conflicts between board members a result of differing opinions or experience on other boards? Address the elephant in the room!

Prayer: "Lord, give us the right hearts and the right motivations to become more effective stewards in our governance roles and responsibilities. Help us to be lifelong learners. Amen."

40 | A Board Prayer

> "Dear God...Let me tell stories and provide statistics that represent accurately."

Dear God,

THANK YOU for calling this ministry into existence and for allowing it to serve and care for the people you love.

- ▶ Thank you for the various perspectives represented in this meeting and the things we will learn from one another.

- ▶ Thank you for the privilege of corporately receiving reports, and with one voice establishing policies, discovering direction, setting goals and encouraging those who serve in this ministry.

- ▶ Thank you for the many people whose lives will be influenced through our meeting—other board members, staff, volunteers, donors, participants, vendors, and generations yet unborn who will benefit from the decisions we make today.

- ▶ And God, thank you for entrusting your ministry into our care. Help us to be worthy of the trust that you and others are placing in us.

Father, allow me to REPORT HONESTLY.

- ▶ Help me to tell the whole truth not just the parts that make me look good.

▶ Let me not bury bad news in mounds of data and detail and don't let me gloss over painful issues or personal failures.

▶ Help me to give credit to others and take responsibility for failure and lack of progress.

▶ Don't let me trivialize serious issues or magnify minor successes.

▶ Let me tell stories and provide statistics that represent accurately.

▶ Help me remember that good information provides a smooth pathway to good decisions.

God, as we approach this meeting, help us to SEE CLEARLY.

▶ Help us to see the issues before us from many perspectives—but ultimately from your perspective. Align our thoughts with your thoughts and our work with your desire.

▶ God, help us to see our ministry's strengths and weaknesses and to embrace both.

▶ Help us connect the dots between the many good ideas to find the great idea you have for us.

▶ Help us to distinguish what is significant from what is superficial,
what is short-term from what is long-term, and
what is best for me from what is best for all.

Help me to LISTEN OBJECTIVELY.

▶ Allow me the grace to filter angry words and hear the truth behind what is being said.

▶ Help me to listen to the painful heart from which flows harsh comments.

▶ Help me to learn from what is legitimate and to discard what is said in spite.

▶ Help me to respond to questions with grace and respect.

▶ Allow me to focus on what is being said more than how I will respond.

Help me to SPEAK CAUTIOUSLY.

▶ Let me use the least words, the least intensity, the least volume needed to be understood.

▶ Help me voice my opinions with care, strength, and meekness.

▶ Help me to ask good questions, open dialogue, explore options, and deepen discussion.

▶ Help me to say nothing degrading and nothing that would draw lines of conflict unnecessarily.

▶ Help me to affirm and agree whenever possible.

▶ Help me to give second voice to a courageous and wise first voice; those who risk presenting a new, contrary, or unrefined perspective.

▶ Lord, help me to accept compliments and approval with humility.

▶ God, give me the grace to watch with dignity as my proposal fails, and give me humility when my idea meets with approval.

Dear God, give the board wisdom to PLAN WISELY.

▶ Help us to see opportunities and threats and to count the cost and to weigh risks and rewards.

▶ Help us to see the possibilities for a better future.

▶ Help us to honor the past but give us the courage to abandon the methods that provided yesterday's success but will lead to futility tomorrow.

▶ Help us discover and employ the most effective methods to accomplish your mission for this ministry in the days ahead.

▶ Help this board to avoid the herd mentality that could stampede the ministry in a dangerous and reckless direction.

▶ Help us to see which decisions are easily reversed and which ones are changed at great peril.

And dear God, help us to REMAIN UNIFIED.

▶ Allow every member to express his or her opinion fully.

▶ Help us to engage the dreams for the future with harmony and enthusiasm.

► Help each of us to leave this meeting with the commitment to speak with one voice and to support the group decisions in public and private.

► Help us to remember that few decisions are worth the divisions caused by dominant winning or belligerent losing.

► Help us to seek your glory and not ours.

► Grant us the joy of arriving at adjournment closer to one another because we are closer to you.

AMEN

"A Board Prayer" by Dan Bolin.[1] © Copyright 2014 by Dan Bolin Resources, Inc. (dan@danbolin.com)

Read this prayer at your next board meeting.

Distribute copies to each board member. One at a time—around the boardroom—ask each board member to read one sentence until the prayer is completed. Then, in teams of two, invite each person to share with their partner the one sentence that the Holy Spirit nudged them about.

STUDY GUIDE

Here are five ways to leverage the insights in this book and enrich the governance experience for your board:

1. **APPOINT A "LEADERS ARE READERS CHAMPION."** Discern which board member has the greatest passion for inspiring your board to be lifelong learners in effective Christ-centered governance. Ask that person to study this book thoroughly in order to keep governance topics and trends on your board's front burner. Ensure that every board member reads at least one governance book a year. (See "Lesson 38: Great Boards Delegate Their Reading.")

2. **HIGHLIGHT THE TOP-5 BOARDROOM LESSONS.** Provide your board a "read-and-reflect" worksheet for the five topics that are most critical for the board to address in the next three to six months. At each board meeting, facilitate a discussion on at least one high-priority topic. (See the next idea.)

3. **INVEST "10 MINUTES FOR GOVERNANCE" IN EVERY BOARD MEETING.** Read Lesson 39 for ideas on how to address each of your Top-5 topics at future board meetings this year. Set a timer for 10 minutes and end promptly at the buzzer. This Governance 101 briefing will engage your board members—and remind them at each meeting that lifelong governance learning is important. Be sure to rotate the leadership so several

board members have the privilege of being 10-minute facilitators.

4. **HIGHLIGHT BOARDROOM LESSONS AT YOUR NEXT RETREAT.** Prior to your next board retreat, give a copy of *Lessons From the Nonprofit Boardroom* to each board member and invite every board member to read and review their favorite lesson. Limit each lesson review to 10 minutes: five minutes for the lesson highlights and five minutes for discussion. Sprinkle the reviews throughout the retreat and have a flipchart ready for listing next steps.

5. **READ "A BOARD PRAYER" TOGETHER.** Follow the facilitation suggestions for "Lesson 40: A Board Prayer." Plus, read "Lesson 10: Prioritize Prayer Over Problems" and learn why one board prays this prayer at every board meeting.

ENDNOTES

Part 1 – The Powerful Impact of Highly Engaged Boards

[1] Richard Kriegbaum, introduction to *Steward Leader Meditations: Fifty Devotions for the Leadership Journey* by R. Scott Rodin (Colbert, WA: Kingdom Life Publishing, 2016), 13.

Lesson 1 – Wanted: Lifelong Learners

[1] Ram Charan, *Owning Up: The 14 Questions Every Board Member Needs to Ask* (San Francisco: John Wiley & Sons, Inc., 2009), 1.

[2] Ibid.

[3] BoardSource, *The Nonprofit Board Answer Book: A Practical Guide for Board Members and Chief Executives*, 3d ed. (San Francisco: Jossey-Bass, 2012).

[4] Charan, *Owning Up*.

[5] Peter Drucker, Frances Hesselbein, and Joan Snyder Kuhl, *Peter Drucker's Five Most Important Questions: Enduring Wisdom for Today's Leaders* (Hoboken, NJ: John Wiley & Sons, 2015).

[6] Bill Hybels, *Leadership Axioms: Powerful Leadership Proverbs* (Grand Rapids, MI: Zondervan, 2008), 196–97.

Lesson 2 – Ask the Gold Standard Question

[1] Henry Cloud, *Necessary Endings: The Employees, Businesses, and Relationships That All of Us Have to Give Up in Order to Move Forward* (New York: Harper Business, 2010), 30–31.

[2] Ibid., 24.

[3] Ibid.

[4] Adapted from John Pearson "The Gold Standard Question for Board Members." Posted September 10, 2015. ECFA: *http://ecfagovernance. blogspot.com/2015/09/the-gold-standard-question-for-board.html*.

[5] BoardSource, *The Nonprofit Board Answer Book*, 141–74.

Lesson 3 – Assess Your Boardroom Demeanor and Engagement

[1] "A Board Prayer," by Dan Bolin, is reprinted by permission in its entirety in Lesson 40.

[2] Bill Hybels, *The Power of a Whisper: Hearing God. Having the Guts to Respond.* (Grand Rapids, MI: Zondervan, 2010), 204–05.

[3] Ibid., 129–30.

Part 2 – Boardroom Tools, Templates, and Typos

[1] Peter F. Drucker, *The Practice of Management* (New York: HarperBusiness, 2006), 135.

Lesson 4 – Do Unwritten Board Policies Really Exist?

[1] Frederic L. Laughlin and Robert C. Andringa, *Good Governance for Nonprofits: Developing Principles and Policies for an Effective Board* (New York: AMACOM, 2007), 174.

[2] Ibid., 179.

[3] Ibid., 31.

[4] Ibid., 45.

Lesson 5 – *Before* the Board Meeting

[1] Max De Pree, *Called to Serve: Creating and Nurturing the Effective Volunteer Board* (Grand Rapids, MI: Wm. B. Eerdmans, 2001), 23.

Lesson 6 – Eliminate Hallway Whining

[1] Gary Keller and Jay Papasan, *The ONE Thing: The Surprisingly Simple Truth Behind Extraordinary Results* (Austin, TX: Bard, 2012), 187.

[2] For more on the four social styles, visit www.socialstyle.com.

Lesson 7 – Typos Matter!

[1] Laura Stevens, "Amazon Finds the Cause of Its AWS Outage: A Typo," Posted March 2, 2017. *The Wall Street Journal: https://www.wsj.com/articles/ amazon-finds-the-cause-of-its-aws-outage-a-typo-1488490506.*

[2] As noted in "Chapter 19: The Printing Bucket," John Pearson, *Mastering the Management Buckets: 20 Critical Competencies for Leading Your Business or Nonprofit* (Ventura, CA: Regal, 2008), 250.

[3] Fred Smith, Sr., *Breakfast with Fred* (Ventura, CA: Regal, 2007).

[4] *The Chicago Manual of Style: The Essential Guide for Writers, Editors, and Publishers,* 17th ed. (Chicago: Univ. of Chicago Press, 2017).

[5] Pearson, *Mastering the Management Buckets,* 251.

Part 3 – Nominees for the Board Member Hall of Fame

Lesson 8 – Listen to the Wisdom of Many Counselors

[1] Richard Kriegbaum, *Leadership Prayers* (Wheaton, IL: Tyndale, 1998), 31.

Lesson 9 – Serve With Humility and Experience God's Presence

[1] Andrew Murray, *Humility: The Beauty of Holiness* (Radford, VA: Wilder, 2008), 9.

[2] E. LeBron Fairbanks, Dwight M. Gunter II, and James R. Couchenour, *Best Practices for Effective Boards* (Kansas City, MO: Beacon Hill, 2012), 57 (quoting General Norman Schwarzkopf).

Lesson 10 – Prioritize Prayer Over Problems

[1] "A Board Prayer," by Dan Bolin, is reprinted by permission in its entirety in Lesson 40. "A Board Prayer" is also included in the book, *TRUST: The Firm Foundation for Kingdom Fruitfulness,* by Dan Busby; and in the facilitator resources for the *ECFA Governance Toolbox No. 3: Conflicts of Interest.*

[2] John Pellowe, *Serving as a Board Member: Practical Guidance for Directors of Christian Ministries* (Elmira, ON, Canada: Canadian Council of Christian Charities, 2012), 46.

[3] Ibid., 46-47.

Part 4 – Epiphanies in the Boardroom

[1] Bruce Bugbee, *What You Do Best in the Body of Christ: Discover Your Spiritual Gifts, Personal Style, and God-Given Passion* (Grand Rapids, MI: Zondervan, 1995), 135 (quoting an unnamed person).

Lesson 11 – *Tap! Tap! Tap!*

[1] Stephen A. Macchia, "Spiritual Discernment: Emerging from a Burning or Burned Out Heart?" *ECFA Focus on Accountability* (Third Quarter 2011), 4.

[2] Stephen A. Macchia, "Restoring Leaders' Souls: Your Spiritual Needs Must Be a Priority," *CLA Outcomes* (Spring 2011), 28–32.

[3] Ruth Haley Barton, *Strengthening the Soul of Your Leadership: Seeking God in the Crucible of Ministry* (Downers Grove, IL: InterVarsity Press, 2008), 67.

[4] Ruth Haley Barton, *Pursuing God's Will Together: A Discernment Practice for Leadership Groups* (Downers Grove, IL: InterVarsity Press, 2012).

Lesson 12 – Vision Growth Must Equal Leader Growth

[1] Charan, *Owning Up*, 70–71.

[2] David L. McKenna, *Stewards of a Sacred Trust: CEO Selection, Transition and Development for Boards of Christ-centered Organizations* (Winchester, VA: ECFAPress, 2010)

[3] Charan, *Owning Up*, 68.

[4] Kriegbaum, *Leadership Prayers*, 113.

Lesson 13 – If You Need a Volunteer, Recruit a Volunteer

[1] Keller and Papasan, *The ONE Thing*, 1–3.

[2] *Chariots of Fire*, directed by Hugh Hudson (1981; United Kingdom: Warner Home Video, 2005), DVD.

[3] Peter F. Drucker, Management: Tasks, Responsibilities, Practices, (New York: HarperBusiness, 1993), 628.

[4] Bugbee, *What You Do Best in the Body of Christ*, 135.

[5] *ECFA Governance Toolbox Series No. 2: Balancing Board Roles— Understanding the 3 Board Hats: Governance, Volunteer, Participant* (Winchester, VA: ECFAPress, 2013), DVD.

Lesson 14 – If You Need a Board Member, Recruit a Board Member

[1] John Carver, *Boards That Make a Difference: A New Design for Leadership in Nonprofit and Public Organizations*, 3d ed. (San Francisco: Jossey-Bass, 2006), 72.

[2] Ralph E. Enlow Jr., *The Leader's Palette: Seven Primary Colors* (Bloomington, IN: WestBow, 2013), 80.

[3] Carver, *Boards That Make a Difference*, 72.

[4] *ECFA Governance Toolbox Series No. 1: Recruiting Board Members—Leveraging the 4 Phases of Board Recruitment: Cultivation, Recruitment, Orientation, Engagement* (Winchester, VA: ECFAPress, 2012) DVD.

[5] Richard T. Ingram, *Ten Basic Responsibilities of Nonprofit Boards*, 3d ed. (Washington, DC: BoardSource, 2015)

[6] John Carver and Miriam Mayhew Carver, *Basic Principles of Policy Governance* (San Francisco: Jossey-Bass, 1996) This is the first of several booklets (each about 25 pages) in *The CarverGuide Series on Effective Governance*.

Part 5 – Boardroom Bloopers

[1] Patrick Lencioni, foreword to *The Imperfect Board Member: Discovering the Seven Disciplines of Governance Excellence*, by Jim Brown (San Francisco: Jossey-Bass, 2006), xi.

Lesson 15 – Cut Your Losses

[1] John C. Maxwell, *Leadership Gold: Lessons I've Learned from a Lifetime of Leading* (Nashville: Thomas Nelson, 2008), 171.

[2] Ibid., 164.

Lesson 16 – Date Board Prospects Before You Propose Marriage

[1] Pellowe, *Serving as a Board Member*, 4–5.

[2] ECFAPress, *ECFA Governance Toolbox Series No. 1*.

[3] Pellowe, *Serving as a Board Member*, 4.

[4] ECFAPress, *ECFA Governance Toolbox Series No. 1*.

Lesson 17 – Sidetrack Harebrained Ideas

[1] Ram Charan, Dennis Carey, and Michael Useem, *Boards That Lead: When to Take Charge, When to Partner, and When to Stay Out of the Way* (Boston: Harvard Business Review Press, 2014), 62.

Lesson 18 – Do Not Interrupt!

[1] Ibid., 61.

[2] Visit www.socialstyle.com and read other resources on social styles including the faith-based book, *How to Deal with Annoying People: What to Do When You Can't Avoid Them*, by Bob Phillips and Kimberly Alyn, and "The People Bucket" chapter in *Mastering the Management Buckets: 20 Critical Competencies for Leading Your Business or Nonprofit*, by John Pearson.

[3] Barton, *Pursuing God's Will Together*, 206–207. Barton adapted these 10 listening guidelines from the book, *Grounded in God*, by Suzanne G. Farnham, Stephanie A. Hull, and R. Taylor McLean.

[4] Ibid., 201.

Part 6 – Boardroom Time-Wasters, Troublemakers, and Truth-Tellers

[1] Charan, Carey and Useem, *Boards That Lead*, 62.

Lesson 19 –Never Throw Red Meat on the Board Table

[1] Cathy Leimbach, "Wording Motions in Advance," Posted March 10, 2017. *Agon Leadership: http://www.agonleadership.com/2017/03/ wording-motions-in-advance/.*

Lesson 20 – Apply for a Staff Position and You Can Deal With That Issue!

[1] Charan, Carey and Useem, *Boards That Lead*, 201.

Lesson 21 – Back Off the Ledge of Dysfunctional Mayhem

[1] Eric Metaxas, *Bonhoeffer: Pastor, Martyr, Prophet, Spy* (Nashville: Thomas Nelson, 2010), 176.

Part 7 – Boardroom Best Practices

[1] Dan Busby, *TRUST: The Firm Foundation for Kingdom Fruitfulness,* rev. ed. (Winchester, VA: ECFAPress, June 2015), 114.

Lesson 22 – The Most Underrated Board Position

[1] David L. McKenna, *Call of the Chair: Leading the Board of the Christ-Centered Ministry* (Winchester, VA: ECFAPress, 2017), 11.

[2] Ibid., 107-19.

[3] Ibid., 117.

[4] Ibid.

Lesson 23 – Focus on Mission Impact *and* Sustainability

[1] Elmer Towns and Warren Bird, *Into the Future: Turning Today's Church Trends Into Tomorrow's Opportunities* (Grand Rapids, MI: Fleming H. Revell, 2000), 14.

[2] Jeanne Bell, Jan Masaoka, and Steve Zimmerman, *Nonprofit Sustainability: Making Strategic Decisions for Financial Sustainability* (San Francisco: Jossey-Bass, 2010), 25.

[3] John R. Frank, *Stewardship as a Lifestyle: Seeking to Live as a Steward and Disciple* (Indianapolis: Dog Ear, 2012), 25.

[4] Busby, *TRUST*, 25.

[5] Bell, Masaoka, and Zimmerman, *Nonprofit Sustainability*, 25.

[6] Drucker, Hesselbein, Kuhl, *Peter Drucker's Five Most Important Questions*, 10.

[7] John Pearson, *Mastering the Management Buckets: 20 Critical Competencies for Leading Your Business or Nonprofit*, 94.

Lesson 24 – Ministry Fundraising 101 for Board Members

[1] For one example of a ministry's gift acceptance policy, visit ECFA.org/Content/Gift-Acceptance-Guidelines in the ECFA Knowledge Center.

[2] "ECFA Standard 7.5 – Stewardship of Charitable Gifts – Percentage Compensation for Securing Charitable Gifts." ECFA: http://www.ecfa.org/Content/Comment75 ("An organization may not base compensation of

outside stewardship resource consultants or its own staff directly or indirectly on a percentage of charitable contributions raised.").

[3] "Position Paper: Percentage-Based Compensation." *AFP: http://www.afpnet.org/ethics/ethicsarticledetail.cfm?itemnumber=734* ("AFP holds that percentage based compensation can encourage abuses, imperils the integrity of the voluntary sector, and undermines the very philanthropic values on which the voluntary sector is based.").

[4] Dan Busby, Michael Martin, and John Van Drunen, *The Guide to Charitable Giving for Churches and Ministries: A Practical Resource on How to Handle Gifts with Integrity* (Winchester, VA: ECFAPress, 2015).

Part 8 – Boardroom Worst Practices

[1] Brian O'Connell, *Board Overboard: Laughs and Lessons for All but the Perfect Nonprofit* (San Francisco: Jossey Bass Inc., Publishers, 1996), xiv.

Lesson 25 – Align Board Member Strengths With Committee Assignments

[1] Pellowe, *Serving as a Board Member*, 19.

[2] Tom Rath, *StrengthsFinder 2.0*, (New York: Gallup Press, 2007).

[3] For more on the four social styles, visit www.socialstyle.com.

[4] Rath, *StrengthsFinder 2.0*, iii.

Lesson 26 – Spotting, Catching, or Exiting a Falling CEO

[1] Charan, Carey, and Useem, *Boards That Lead*, 139.

Lesson 27 – Report Once and Report With Clarity

[1] Fred Laughlin and Bob Andringa, authors of *Good Governance for Nonprofits*, offer helpful guidelines for characteristics of good board reports at amacombooks.org/downloads/good-gov-nonprofits/.

Part 9 – Holy Ground and Other Locations

Lesson 28 – Slow Down and Wait on God

[1] Lorne C. Sanny, *How to Spend a Day in Prayer*, rev. ed. (Colorado Springs, CO: NavPress, 1974), 3.

[2] Barton, *Strengthening the Soul of Your Leadership*, 198.

[3] Sanny, *How to Spend a Day in Prayer*, 4.

[4] Ibid., 20

Lesson 29 – Think and Pray Outside the Box—and the County

[1] Gary G. Hoag, R. Scott Rodin, and Wesley K. Willmer, *The Choice: The Christ-Centered Pursuit of Kingdom Outcomes* (Winchester, VA: ECFAPress, 2014), 31.

[2] Adapted from: "Your Big Holy Audacious Goal," *CCCA Executive Briefing by Bob Kobielush,* Vol. 5, No.8 (August 2007). Used by permission.

[3] Visit JimCollins.com for more on *Built to Last, Good to Great, Good to Great and the Social Sectors, How the Mighty Fall, Great by Choice,* and other books and resources.

[4] Hoag, Rodin, and Willmer, *The Choice*, 31.

[5] Randon A. Samelson, *Breakthrough: Unleashing the Power of a Proven Plan* (Colorado Springs: Counsel & Capital, 2014).

Lesson 30 – The Truck Driver Was No Match for the Faith-Filled Board Chair

[1] Max De Pree, *Called to Serve*, 21.

[2] David La Piana, *The Nonprofit Strategy Revolution: Real-Time Strategic Planning in a Rapid-Response World* (USA: Fieldstone Alliance, 2008), 3.

[3] R. Scott Rodin and Gary G. Hoag, *The Sower: Redefining the Ministry of Raising Kingdom Resources,* (Winchester, VA: ECFAPress, 2010).

Part 10 – Building a 24/7 Board Culture

[1] Fairbanks, Gunter, and Couchenour, *Best Practices for Effective Boards*, 86. The authors attribute Packer Thomas Certified Public Accountants & Business Consultants with adopting the brilliant company motto: "In the long run, only integrity matters. In fact, without integrity, there will be no long run."

Lesson 31 – Cut the Cord! Invite Board Members to Exit When They Don't Live Your Values

[1] De Pree, *Called to Serve*, 73.

[2] *ECFA Governance Survey* (Winchester, VA: ECFAPress, 2012), 16–17.

[3] George Barna and Bill Dallas, *Master Leaders: Revealing Conversations with 30 Leadership Greats* (Carol Stream, IL: BarnaBooks, 2009), 47.

[4] Jack Welch and Suzy Welch, *Winning: The Answers: Confronting 74 of the Toughest Questions in Business Today* (New York: HarperCollins, 2006), 57.

[5] Ibid., 58.

[6] Bill Thrall, Bruce McNicol, and John Lynch, *TrueFaced: Trust God and Others With Who You Really Are* (Colorado Spring: NavPress, 2003), 196.

Lesson 32 – Loose Lips Sink the Boardroom Ship

[1] Laughlin and Andringa, *Good Governance for Nonprofits*, 114–15. The authors recommend a Board Members' Code of Conduct, including confidentiality, be addressed in the board policies manual.

Lesson 33 – "Good Is the Enemy of Great"

[1] Jim Collins, *Good to Great and the Social Sectors; Why Business Thinking Is Not the Answer* (Boulder, Co: Jim Collins, 2005), 9.

[2] Jim Collins, *Good to Great: Why Some Companies Make the Leap...and Others Don't* (New York: HarperCollins, 2001), 1.

Part 11 – Boards That Lead and Boards That Read

[1] Hybels, *Leadership Axioms*, 196–197.

Lesson 34 – Envision Your Best Board Member Orientation Ever

[1] Patrick Lencioni, foreword to *The Imperfect Board Member*, by Jim Brown, xi.

[2] Michael E. Batts, *Board Member Orientation: The Concise and Complete Guide to Nonprofit Board Service* (Orlando: Accountability Press, 2011), i.

[3] *ECFA Governance Toolbox Series No. 1: Recruiting Board Members.*

Lesson 35 – Is Your Board Color-Blind?

[1] For an excellent guide to growing in discernment as a board, see *Pursuing God's Will Together* by Ruth Haley Barton.

Lesson 36 – Decrease Staff Reporting and Increase Heavy Lifting

[1] Joey Asher, *15 Minutes Including Q&A: A Plan to Save the World from Lousy Presentations* (Atlanta: Persuasive Speaker Press, 2010), 49.

[2] Ibid., 1.

[3] Eugene H. Fram with Vicki Brown, *Going for Impact: The Nonprofit Director's Essential Guidebook* (Self-published: CreateSpace, 2016), 103.

[4] For more on the four social styles, visit www.socialstyle.com.

Lesson 37 – Don't Stretch Credulity With BHAGs and Stretch Goals

[1] Charan, Carey, and Useem, *Boards That Lead*, 139.

[2] Sim B. Sitkin, C. Chet Miller, and Kelly E. See, "The Stretch Goal Paradox." Posted January 2017. *Harvard Business Review: https://hbr.org/2017/01/the-stretch-goal-paradox.*

[3] Ibid.

[4] James C. Collins and Jerry I. Porras, *Built to Last: Successful Habits of Visionary Companies* (New York: HarperCollins, 1994), 91. (The authors describe BHAGs as "Big Hairy Audacious Goals" in Chapter 5.)

[4] Barton, *Pursuing God's Will Together*, 99.

Lesson 38 – Great Boards Delegate Their Reading

[1] John Ortberg, *The Life You've Always Wanted: Spiritual Disciplines for Ordinary People* (Grand Rapids, MI: Zondervan, 1997), 188.

[2] Jeffrey A. Sonnenfeld, "What Makes Great Boards Great." Posted September 2002. *Harvard Business Review: https://hbr.org/2002/09/what-makes-great-boards-great.*

Lesson 39 – Invest "10 Minutes for Governance" in Every Board Meeting

[1] Richard Kriegbaum, introduction to *Steward Leader Meditations* by R. Scott Rodin, 13.

[2] *ECFA Governance Toolbox Series No. 2: Balancing Board Roles.*

[3] Hybels, *Leadership Axioms*, 196.

[4] Barton, *Pursuing God's Will Together*, 207.

[5] Fairbanks, Gunter II, and Couchenour, *Best Practices for Effective Boards*, 178–179.

Lesson 40 – A Board Prayer

[1] The authors are grateful to Dan Bolin for sharing this prayer with leaders and board members of Christ-centered ministries. As the International Director of Christian Camping International, www.cciworldwide.org, the Lord inspired Dan to write this humbling prayer while serving board members during an overseas trip. The prayer is also included, by permission, in the book, *TRUST: The Firm Foundation for Kingdom Fruitfulness*, published by ECFAPress and is available at www.ecfa.org/ECFAPress.aspx. In addition, the prayer is included as a resource to supplement the materials in the *ECFA Governance Toolbox Series No. 3: Conflicts of Interest—Addressing Board and Organizational Conflicts of Interest: Avoiding Trouble, Trouble, Trouble With Related-Party Transactions* (http://www.ecfa.org/Toolbox).

INDEX

ABOUT THE AUTHORS

DAN BUSBY

Dan Busby is the President of ECFA (Evangelical Council for Financial Accountability) in Winchester, VA. He has been in leadership positions with ECFA for nearly 20 years. Prior to coming to ECFA, Dan was the founding and managing partner of a CPA firm in the Kansas City area, served in financial management positions with the University of Kansas Medical Center and The Wesleyan Church—International Headquarters. He has served over 110 man-years on nonprofit boards.

Dan is the author/co-author of 62 editions of eight different titles plus numerous eBooks and booklets. Two titles published annually since 1991, the *Zondervan Minister's Tax & Financial Guide* and the *Zondervan Church and Financial Guide*, have set a standard as easy-to-understand resources on these topics.

His recent book, *TRUST: The Firm Foundation for Kingdom Fruitfulness* is a treasure trove linked to trust, based on Busby's wit and wisdom. Joined by co-authors Michael Martin and John Van Drunen, *The Guide to Charitable Giving for Churches and Ministries* answers the important questions about the proper handling of charitable contributions for legal, tax, and accounting purposes.

An avid baseball fan and former umpire, Dan frequently consults with the National Baseball Hall of Fame concerning memorabilia acquisitions. His books about the Brooklyn Dodgers and New York Yankees, based on their tickets and passes, are scheduled for release in 2018.

Dan, and his wife, Claudette, have two children, Julie and Alan, and two grandchildren. His top five strengths in the Gallup StrengthsFinder assessment are: Learner, Achiever, Connectedness, Ideation, and Belief. A survivor of living in "tornado alley" in Kansas until 1987, Dan has not sought shelter from tornadoes since leaving Kansas.

JOHN PEARSON

John Pearson is a board governance and management consultant from San Clemente, CA. He served more than 30 years as a nonprofit ministry CEO, 25 of those years as the CEO of three national/international associations, including Willow Creek Association, Christian Camp and Conference Association, and Christian Management Association (now Christian Leadership Alliance).

He is the author of *Mastering the Management Buckets: 20 Critical Competencies for Leading Your Business or Nonprofit,* and the co-author with Dr. Robert Hisrich of *Marketing Your Ministry: 10 Critical Principles.*

John also writes an eNewsletter, *Your Weekly Staff Meeting*, and since 2006, he has reviewed more than 350 leadership and management books in his eNews. He writes a board blog for ECFA, "Governance of Christ-Centered Organizations," and is the creator of the *ECFA Governance Toolbox Series*. John also served five years as the lead facilitator of the M.J. Murdock Charitable Trust's Board Leadership & Development Program. He currently serves as the board chair of Christian Community Credit Union.

John and his wife, Joanne, have traveled and/or facilitated leadership, management and board governance training in more than 50 countries and are blessed to live close to their son, Jason, and daughter-in-law, Melinda, and their five grandchildren (including triplet teenagers). His top five strengths in the Gallup StrengthsFinder assessment are: Focus, Responsibility, Significance, Belief, and Maximizer. A survivor of 21 winters in Chicago, John has not shoveled snow since 1994.

John's website is: www.ManagementBuckets.com.

ABOUT ECFA

Enhancing Trust

ECFA enhances trust in Christ-centered churches and ministries by establishing and applying Seven Standards of Responsible Stewardship™ to accredited organizations.

Founded in 1979, ECFA provides accreditation to leading Christian nonprofit organizations that faithfully demonstrate compliance with established standards for financial accountability, transparency, fundraising, and board governance. The Christ-centered ministries accredited by ECFA include churches, denominations, educational institutions, rescue missions, camps, and many other types of tax-exempt 501(c)(3) organizations. Collectively, these organizations represent over $27 billion in annual revenue.

ECFA accreditation entitles a ministry to use the ECFA seal and receive other Accreditation Benefits. The continuing use of the seal depends on the ministry's good faith compliance with all ECFA Standards.

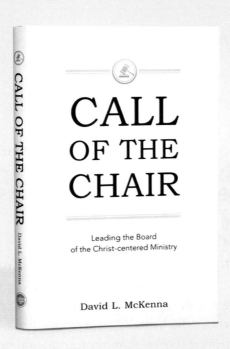

As Christ-centered ministries go through changing times, the leadership role of the board chair rises in significance. As manager of the board, the chair joins the CEO in responsibility for advancing the mission, partnering with the vision, governing by policy, and setting the tone for the morale of the ministry. Such leadership requires a chair who is appointed by God, gifted with integrity, trust and humility, and anointed by the Holy Spirit.

With deft strokes written out of learning from professional practice, understanding from spiritual discipline, and insight from personal experience, David McKenna leaves no doubt. Unless chosen by God, the chair will fail; unless gifted with integrity, trust and humility, the board will fail; and unless obedient to the Spirit, the ministry will fail. Loud and clear, the message is sent to every Christ-centered ministry: The call of the chair is the call of God.

Place your order at
ECFA.org/ECFAPress.aspx

GOVERNANCE TOOLBOX DIGITAL SERIES

Just-In-Time Help and Inspiration!

SHORT VIDEO + 10 MINUTE DISCUSSION = ENGAGEMENT

SERIES No. 1
RECRUITING BOARD MEMBERS

SERIES No. 2
BALANCING BOARD ROLES

SERIES No. 3
CONFLICTS OF INTEREST

SERIES No. 4
SUCCESSION PLANNING

ENGAGE YOUR BOARD AT EVERY MEETING!
WATCH FOR NEW SERIES TITLES TO INSPIRE & EQUIP YOUR BOARD

Each Toolbox includes:
1 online video,
Board Member Read-and-Engage Viewing Guide *(pdf download)* and
Facilitator Guide *(pdf download)*

ORDER RESOURCES FROM: ECFA.ORG/TOOLBOX

VIEW • INSPIRE • ENGAGE!